CONTENTS

Published by Thomas Cook Publishing
The Thomas Cook Group Ltd
PO Box 227, Thorpe Wood
Peterborough PE3 6PU
United Kingdom

Telephone: 01733 503571
E-mail: books@thomascook.com

ISBN 1 841570 72 9

Distributed in the United States of America by the Globe Pequot Press,
PO Box 480, Guilford, Connecticut 06437, USA.

Distributed in Canada by Whitecap Books, 351 Lynn Avenue,
North Vancouver, British Columbia, Canada V7J 2C4.

Distributed in Australia and New Zealand by Peribo Pty Limited,
58 Beaumont Road, Mt Kuring-Gai, NSW, 2080, Australia.

Publisher: Stephen York
Commissioning Editor: Deborah Parker
Map Editor: Bernard Horton

Series Editor: Christopher Catling

Written and researched by: Christopher Catling and Tony Kelly
(Practical information by Lucy Thomson)

Cover photograph: Ethel Davies

must-see LONDON

CHRISTOPHER CATLING
and TONY KELLY

Getting to know London

GETTING TO KNOW LONDON

Discovering London

The eyes of the world were on London on 31 December 1999 as Big Ben struck midnight to welcome the new millennium. As the home of the Greenwich Meridian and therefore of time itself, London, more than anywhere else, has taken on the role of the world's Millennium City.

The city has grasped the opportunity to reinvent itself with some stunning modern architecture. The world's largest observation wheel, the London Eye, now lights up the skyline; a huge dome stands on the Greenwich peninsula beside the Thames. The river, for so long the lifeblood of London, has returned to centre stage, with new bridges, footpaths, riverboats and piers. Along its South Bank, a redundant power station has been reborn as an art gallery and a building to house London's new government is taking shape beside Tower Bridge.

In short, at the start of the 21st century, London is feeling good about itself. The city has had a buzz about it for several years, ever since *Newsweek* dubbed London the coolest place on the planet. Before long, everyone was talking about **Cool Britannia**. In practice, it meant little more than a few trendy artists, a celebrity chef or two and a young, popular Prime Minister who happened to like rock music. It may have been a piece of hype dreamed up by the marketing gurus, but a label had been born – and it has stuck.

Steeped in tradition

Yet as those who live in this great city know, what is fascinating about London is not that it is hip but that it is both forward-looking and deeply traditional at the same time. This is a city that has learnt to welcome change while remaining acutely conscious of its own heritage. Where else do you find the pageantry of Trooping the Colour, or the Changing of the Queen's Guard? Where else do politicians and lawyers dress up in ridiculous costumes and enact theatrical rituals in arcane language? Which other great financial centre is presided over by a Lord Mayor, chosen from the liveried ranks of the medieval guilds?

London wears its history on every street corner, with statues of forgotten statesmen and memorials to missionaries and explorers. Monuments to previous generations are everywhere, recalling this benefactor or that clergyman who founded such-and-such a hospital or school. The past lives on in the city's churches, designed by Sir Christopher Wren amid the ruins of the Great Fire, and in the names of the streets (Cheapside, Poultry, Haymarket) which recall London's role as a medieval centre of trade.

Endless possibilities

London is a city on a global scale. It has more theatres than New York and more artists than Paris. It has cutting-edge restaurants, magnificent parks, vibrant nightlife, elegant squares, chic shops, fascinating museums and some of the finest art galleries in the world. It is almost impossible to be bored here. Clichéd it may be, and endlessly repeated, but there is still a great deal of truth in Dr Johnson's celebrated *bon mot*.

> *"When a man is tired of London, he is tired of life; for there is in London all that life can afford."*
>
> **Dr Samuel Johnson (1709–84)**

Life in London

The pattern of London life has changed in recent years because people now live in the city once more.

Back in 1939, when London was the biggest city in the world (population 8.6 million), war and the Blitz destroyed many homes and drove Londoners out to new 'overspill' towns. Others moved out in the post-war era in search of the good life in commuter towns and cities as far away as Oxford and Brighton. For 50 years, London's population declined, while commuter traffic grew to 1.25 million people a day.

In the 1990s, the tide began to turn. Despite an astonishing escalation in house prices, city living is now considered cool again and people want to be as close to the centre as possible. London no longer closes down after dark or at weekends. Instead it buzzes with vibrant life, as Londoners throng the streets at night, joined by the 23 million visitors who come here every year from all over the globe.

London dawning

London is still a late-rising city, with stores not opening their doors until 1000, which is when most offices also begin to function. Exceptions are **the City** trading desks, where brokers specialising in the Far East start work in the cold light of dawn. A short step from the City's financial hub, **Smithfield meat market** is in full swing and has been since midnight. By 0800, hungry traders and porters in bloodstained aprons will sit down to eat gargantuan 'breakfasts' (in reality, their supper) alongside City workers enjoying their first coffee of the day.

London after dark

At the other end of the day, those who still **commute** will pack into overcrowded underground trains and hurry to one of the mainline commuter stations, anxious not to miss their train, but knowing that it is quite likely to be delayed or cancelled. For Londoners, the antiquated state of the public transport system is a major misery and its modernisation will be a key test of competence for the city's new mayor.

The lucky ones who don't commute may work until 1900 before joining friends at a pub, club, theatre, concert hall or cinema. Late-opening record stores, such as Virgin, HMV and Tower Records, have become popular social centres, as have bookshops, such as Waterstones and Borders, where intellectual singles hope to meet like-minded souls browsing amongst the travel books or sipping coffee in the in-store café.

The restaurant scene

Many young and unencumbered Londoners now dine out regularly – as often as two or three nights a week – a trend that has revolutionised the London restaurant scene. Once culinarily challenged, London now has the **biggest range of cuisines** to be found in any European capital, ranging from Thai to Californian fusion and New Wave Tuscan.

Fashionable London will party on past midnight at clubs and discos, but working Londoners keep an eye on the clock so as not to miss the last of the late-night tubes. Many will go home to bedsits in suburban Clapham, or Balham, dreaming of the day they will be able to afford a Manhattan-style loft in the Docklands, or in some converted factory or office block on the City fringes.

Yesterday and tomorrow

Archaeologists who were called in recently to investigate some rotting timbers in the mud of the Thames were astonished to find the remains of an 8th-century BC Bronze-Age causeway. Here, in the shadow of Vauxhall Bridge, was evidence that London was far, far older than anyone had ever imagined.

The Thames was once much wider and shallower than it is now, comprising numerous water channels intersected by low, tree-covered islands. The **Romans** had to negotiate this river when they invaded Britain in AD 43. They built the first of several bridges on the site of today's London Bridge and used it to push north to defeat Cunobelin (Shakespeare's Cymbeline) at his stronghold in Colchester. Led by **Boudicca** (Boadicea), the British struck back in AD 60, taking advantage of the Roman army's absence to sack the new city, setting fire to the buildings and massacring all the inhabitants.

Fire and war

Boudicca's victory was short-lived, for the Roman army returned to wreak vengeance, killing 80,000 British for the cost of 400 Roman lives. The rebuilt city never looked back – instead it expanded westwards. **Saxon invaders** robbed it for building materials and settled on the green fields beneath today's Covent Garden. Further west still, **Edward the Confessor** built a magnificent new abbey at Westminster, with a royal palace (today's Houses of Parliament) alongside.

A city divided

From that time on, London consisted of two distinct parts, with **Westminster** as the centre of government and **the City** as the centre of commerce. In between were the Inns of Court, the forerunners of today's business schools, where the lawyers and civil servants needed to support an increasingly sophisticated city received their training.

London was then a city of timber with one or two prestigious palaces and churches of brick or stone. All was swept away in 1666, when the **Great Fire of London** raged for three days, razing the City to the ground. Camped in the fields around the smouldering ruins of their city, Londoners agreed that they wanted to rebuild their homes as quickly as possible.

Because of the complex pattern of land-holding, Sir Christopher Wren's visionary plan to create a magnificent modern city of wide avenues and classically inspired public buildings came to nothing. The City was rebuilt along medieval lines, cramped alleys and all, but further west no such constraints prevented comprehensive redevelopment of fields and orchards along the Strand and Piccadilly and around Mayfair and St James's. London became one huge building site and has continued to be ever since – 'a wonderful city', as the saying goes, 'if they ever get round to finishing it!'.

Millennium wonders

And the building goes on. Lottery money and the millennium have given new momentum to the process of constant renewal. London has a mayor again, and its own city government after a gap of 14 years. New bridges are planned for the Thames, old buildings are being turned into new homes or museums and the **Docklands** has been transformed into a 21st-century commercial hub. All this greatly enriches an already rich city … and makes it impossible for anyone to claim that they already know London.

People and places

The end-of-millennium building boom has allowed a number of modern architects to flourish.

Chief among them is **Norman Foster**, designer of Stansted Airport, the Millennium Bridge, Canary Wharf station and the new Greater London Authority headquarters at Tower Bridge. **Richard Rogers**, who like Foster has been appointed to the House of Lords, is responsible for the futurist Lloyds Building in the City and also the Millennium Dome. Less well known is **Terry Farrell**, architect of the Charing Cross Station extension and of more London buildings than Sir Christopher Wren. Among his latest plans is a pedestrian boulevard linking Trafalgar Square with Hyde Park and cutting through the gardens of Buckingham Palace.

Cool Britannia

The modern architects are all part of the Cool Britannia phenomenon, epitomised by **Sir Terence Conran**, the style guru who has revolutionised London's dining scene by converting old warehouses and garages into trendy restaurants where the art matters as much as the food. This in turn has spawned a new generation of celebrity chef-owners, such as **Gordon Ramsay** and **Marco Pierre White**, as well as **Damien Hirst**, *enfant terrible* of BritArt and now a restaurateur.

Blue plaques

As you walk around London, keep an eye out for blue plaques, marking the houses of famous former residents. Areas particularly rich in blue plaques include Chelsea, Kensington, Marylebone and Mayfair.

Politics and power

Tony Blair, Prime Minister since 1997, is often accused of jumping on the Cool Britannia bandwagon in an effort to rebrand Britain in his image. One politician who refuses to modernise is **Ken Livingstone**, former leader of the Greater London Council. Despite his left-wing rhetoric and espousal of unpopular causes, 'Red Ken' is held in affection by many Londoners and is the people's choice for mayor.

Historic Londoners

Some people are famous just for being Londoners. **Samuel Pepys** (1633–1703) is best known for his diaries, which reveal much about 17th-century London as well as his own colourful love life and give us a first-hand account of the Great Fire. The lexicographer **Dr Samuel Johnson** (1709–84) has given us keen insights into the life of 18th-century London, especially through his biographer James Boswell. **Charles Dickens** (1812–70), the novelist who wrote *A Christmas Carol* and *Oliver Twist*, is famous for his vivid accounts of the misery and poverty of Victorian London.

Cockneys, cabbies and Pearly Kings

According to tradition, the only true Londoners are **cockneys**, born within the sound of the 'Bow bells' at St Mary-le-Bow Church. Cockneys are known for their authentic London accents and their use of 'rhyming slang', a dialect by which, for example, 'stairs' become 'apples and pears' or even just 'apples'. Cockneys traditionally work as **cabbies** (taxi drivers), renowned for their encyclopaedic knowledge and trenchant views. Another cockney tradition is that of the **Pearly Kings and Queens**, community leaders who dress in pearl-covered cloaks at such events as the annual Costermongers' Harvest Festival, held at St Martin-in-the-Fields in Trafalgar Square each October.

Getting around

Travelcard

Most Londoners get about quickly and easily by public transport and once you have mastered the system it is convenient and relatively cheap to use. Taxis are useful for late-night travelling and getting to out-of-the-way places, but most of the time you should stick to buses and the 'tube' (underground railway). If you are going to be doing much travelling, get hold of a **Travelcard**, valid on buses, the underground and the Docklands Light Railway (DLR). A one-day pass, available at any underground station, can be used after 0930; weekly and monthly Travelcards, for which you need a validated Photocard, can be bought at underground stations and some newsagents and may be used at any time of day or night. Children under five travel free and those under 16 pay reduced fares. For the purpose of calculating fares, the bus and underground systems are divided into zones, with most of London's main attractions lying within the central zone 1.

The tube

If possible, avoid the **rush hours** (approximately 0800–1000 and 1600–1900 on weekdays), when the trains are crowded with 'strap-hanging' commuters, but at other times the tube is reliable and reasonably comfortable. It runs from around 0530–0030 daily, with trains every few minutes on most lines. Harry Beck's underground map, published in 1933, is a London institution, still used with minor modifications today. The colour-coded system allows you to plot your journey and work out where you need to change trains. For occasional central journeys, buy a carnet of ten zone 1 tickets, giving discounted travel within the Circle Line area and to Waterloo and London Bridge on the South Bank.

Docklands Light Railway

This computerised **monorail** system, part of the underground network, opened in 1987. A ride on the DLR is an attraction in its own right, as the train travels high above the houses on its journey from the City, giving spectacular views of Canary Wharf and the Millennium Dome. You can now buy a **'Sail & Rail' ticket** for a round trip to Greenwich by riverboat and DLR.

Buses

Compared to the underground, buses are slow but scenic. For many people, travelling on the top deck of a **double-decker London bus** is the most delightful way to see the city; for others, it is a slow and frustrating crawl through the traffic. On modern one-crew buses, you board at the front and buy your ticket from the driver; on more traditional Routemasters, you board at the back and a conductor comes around to take your fare.

London's bus routes are complicated, but you can pick up a map at the London Transport information centre inside Piccadilly Circus underground station. The map also includes details of **night buses**, which operate from around 2300–0600 daily. As virtually all night buses pass through Trafalgar Square, this is the place to head if you are stuck in central London late at night.

For a scenic tour of London's main sights, take bus 11 from Chelsea to the City, passing Westminster, Trafalgar Square and St Paul's Cathedral. Alternatively, several companies offer tours of London using open-top buses with guided commentaries. These include the **Big Bus Company** (*tel: (020) 7233 9533*), **London Pride** (*tel: (020) 7904 4761*) and **The Original London Sightseeing Tour** (*tel: (020) 8877 1722*). The hop-on, hop-off ticket, valid for 24 hours, usually includes added extras such as a boat cruise and free or discounted entry to attractions. Buy your ticket wherever you see the buses; all of the routes pass through Trafalgar Square.

Boats

After being ignored for many years, the River Thames is returning to use as a valuable public transport resource and there are likely to be more ferry routes operating over the next few years. Already, in addition to **pleasure cruises**, there are fast ferry services linking the north and south banks between Embankment and Canary Wharf (*see pages 52–3*). Another option in summer, and on winter weekends, is a **narrowboat cruise** on the Regent's Canal between Camden Lock and Little Venice via London Zoo (*tel: (020) 7482 2550*).

Taxis

London's 'black cab' drivers are renowned for their knowledge of the city's streets; they are not allowed to operate until they have passed a detailed exam. You can hire a **licensed** taxi from a cab rank (outside stations and hotels) or by hailing it on the street when the yellow **'For Hire' sign** is illuminated. The driver is obliged to take you to your destination by the most direct route, unless you specify otherwise. **Fares** are based on a combination of distance and time travelled, so they can mount up quickly in heavy traffic. There are extra charges for late-night and weekend journeys and for luggage and extra passengers. Drivers will always expect a tip, though this is not compulsory. If you have any complaints, make a note of the driver's serial number and call the Public Carriage Office (*tel: (020) 7230 1631*). As a rule, it is best to avoid unlicensed cabs.

Walking

Although you need to take care when crossing the streets, walking is a great way to see London. On foot, you appreciate the geography of the city; everything is so much closer together than it seems when you travel by tube. All you really need are an *A–Z* and a good pair of shoes, but if you want a guide there are several companies offering walks. The best established is **London Walks** (*tel: (020) 7624 3978; www.walks.com*), whose **themed walks** range from Jack the Ripper to Shakespeare and Princess Diana to Chelsea pubs. There is no need to book – just find out when a walk is taking

place and turn up at the relevant tube station. Other companies offering guided walks include **Historical Walks** (*tel: (020) 8668 4019*) and **Stepping Out** (*tel: (020) 8881 2933*). The classic London walk is the **Thames Path** (*see pages 136–7*), which can be followed from Greenwich to Hampton Court in around two days.

Cycling

The **London Bicycle Tour Company** (*tel: (020) 7928 6838*), at Gabriel's Wharf on the South Bank, offers mountain bikes, children's bikes and traditional cycles for hire and also has a programme of guided half-day and full-day bike rides on safe, relatively traffic-free routes.

Don't miss

1 British Museum

Archaeological treasures from around the world, from the exquisite garnet-encrusted royal regalia of the Sutton Hoo ship burial, to giant narrative friezes from Assyria, not to mention the celebrated Parthenon frieze, which Greece would rather like to have returned. **Page 80**

2 Covent Garden

Packed into the narrow streets surrounding the former fruit market are scores of tiny specialist shops and restaurants, selling everything from buttons and beads and oriental crafts to cutting-edge fashion, furniture and art. Enjoy the free entertainment provided by busking clowns and musicians and visit a clutch of unusual museums. **Page 94**

3 Hampton Court

Great for a day out of town, Henry VIII's vast riverside palace is surrounded by beautiful Tudor gardens and a famous maze. **Page 158**

4 National Gallery

Built up in the 19th century when Renaissance art was out of fashion, the National Gallery's collection, housed in the Sainsbury Wing, is the best outside of Italy. In the main gallery the full riches of post-Renaissance art are displayed and nearly every picture is a winner. **Page 98**

5 Natural History Museum

From the frighteningly realistic dinosaurs (brought to life by animatronics), to the giant bugs in the Creepie Crawlies gallery, thrills abound in this massive museum. Animal and insect life is treated exhaustively in the main museum, while the Earth Galleries tell the story of our planet, from the Big Bang to the Kobe earthquake. **Page 26**

6 Science Museum

Forget school science: this is a fun museum that teaches as it entertains, very popular with children for its interactive displays, and as good on the basics of science as on the glamorous topics of spaceflight, the Internet and the theory of relativity. **Page 28**

7 Tate Gallery x 2

This art gallery is split over two London sites. Modern art from all over the world is found in Tate Modern at Bankside – a stunning conversion of a former power station worth visiting for the building and the views alone. British Art from 1500 to the present day – including the huge Turner bequest – is found at Tate Britain in the original Millbank building. **Pages 47 and 132**

8 Tower of London

Province of the Beefeaters, with their cheerful uniforms of scarlet and gold, it is easy to forget that this was a prison and execution ground, where the ghosts of Sir Walter Raleigh, the Little Princes and a couple of Henry VIII's wives flit across the green, past visitors queuing to see the Crown Jewels. **Page 116**

9 Victoria and Albert Museum

From Indian textiles to 20th-century fashion, and from medieval stained glass to paintings by Constable and Turner, the theme of the decorative arts is interpreted very broadly in this giant museum, where you never quite know what to expect each time you turn a corner. **Page 30**

10 Westminster Abbey

Mix with the shades of dead authors in Poets' Corner, or mingle with deceased royalty in the beautiful Henry VII chapel, where Tudor monarchs lie beneath an exquisite fan vault. Don't miss the funerary waxworks in the crypt – more evocative than anything to be found in Madame Tussaud's. **Page 48**

Knightsbridge and Kensington

Kensington is renowned for its palatial museums – the Victoria and Albert, Science and Natural History Museums – plus the Grecian extravagance of the Albert Hall. Knightsbridge offers the allure of Harrods and Harvey Nichols – department stores as lavishly stocked as any museum.

KNIGHTSBRIDGE AND KENSINGTON

BEST OF

Knightsbridge and Kensington

Getting there: for the museums, take the ***tube*** *to South Kensington and follow the directions through the underpass to avoid crossing busy roads above ground. For the shops, go to Knightsbridge tube and turn left at the exit for Harrods, right for Harvey Nichols, or head down Sloane Street for* bijou *boutiques selling designer label clothes.* ***Buses:*** *Nos 14 and 74 serve both Knightsbridge and Kensington.*

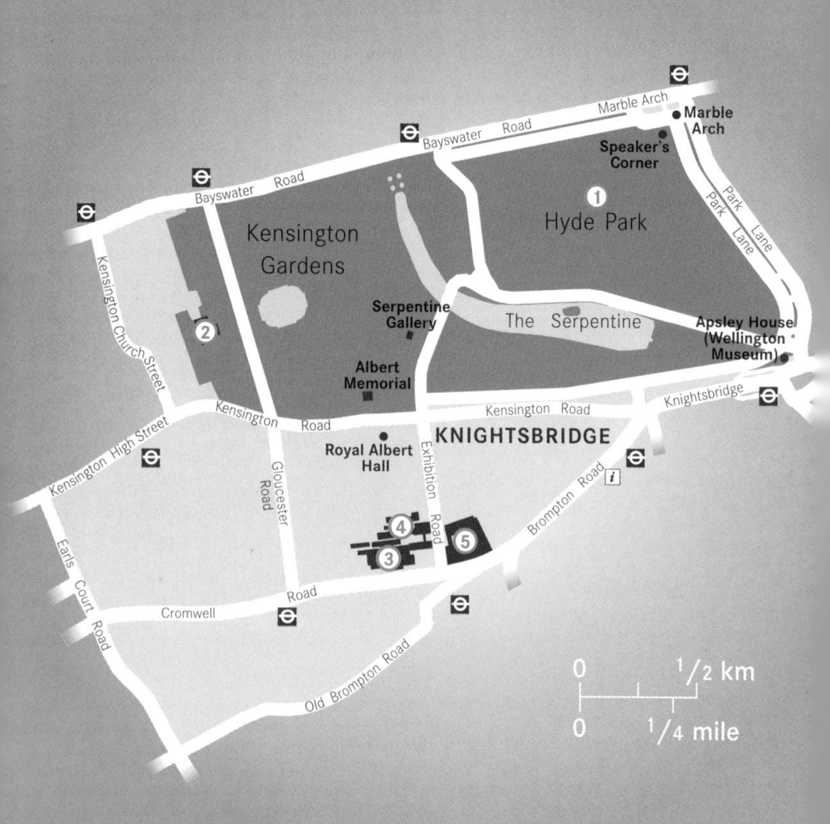

① *Hyde Park*

London's green lung is a great place for jogging at dawn, displaying your roller blading skills, chilling out in a deckchair with a good book, feeding the birds, swimming in the ice-cold Serpentine in the middle of winter, haranguing the crowds at Speaker's Corner or any of the other eccentric outdoor activities that Londoners delight in. **Page 24**

② *Kensington Palace*

Princess Diana's London home, familiar from newscasts of mountains of flowers laid by mourners after her death. Inside the Palace, see the Queen's dresses and other examples of court dress, and visit the room where Queen Victoria was born. **Page 25**

③ *Natural History Museum*

London's number one museum for children and a great place for adults too. Marvel at the iridescent beauty of butterflies and beetles, the astonishing complexity of the rainforest ecosystem or the sheer variety of life on earth. **Pages 26–7**

④ *Science Museum*

Another great children's museum, worth at least a day of anyone's time: head for the Launch Pad for robust hands-on experiments that look like magic but have a rational explanation – if your kids will stick around long enough to hear it. **Pages 28–9**

⑤ *Victoria and Albert Museum*

A museum for which the term serendipity was invented: impossible to sum up and full of fascinating human artefacts that evoke admiration and pleasure: just wander and allow yourself to be surprised. **Pages 30–1**

Shopping

Sniff the truffles in Harvey Nichols food store, shop for lingerie in Beauchamp Place, or check out the Harrods store guide to see what author signings are taking place today.

Tip

The Kensington Museums are very crowded during the school holidays, so arrive early to avoid queuing for admission and to enjoy a relatively quiet first hour or so. The restaurants and cafés are equally busy, so time your visits to avoid the peak lunch period (1200–1400), or leave the museum (your ticket is valid for the day and will readmit you on your return) and sample the food around South Kensington tube station, where there is a Japanese fast-food café and a Polish restaurant among the coffee shops, pizzerias, fish and chip shops and sandwich bars.

Apsley House (The Wellington Museum)

149 Piccadilly, Hyde Park Corner. Tel: (020) 7499 5676. Open: Tue–Sun 1100–1630 (last entry); closed Mon except Bank Holidays; closed Good Friday, May Day, 24–26 Dec and 1 Jan. £.

When Wellington defeated Napoleon at Waterloo (in 1815), a grateful nation granted him £200,000, which he lavished on this marvellous example of Robert Adam's opulent interior design. Wellington filled the house with magnificent paintings (not a few of them looted during the course of his campaigns) by the likes of Velázquez, Goya and Rubens. Even in defeat, Napoleon still manages to be the star of the show: the diminutive French emperor is portrayed nude in Canova's heroic statue, standing at the base of the staircase.

Hyde Park and Kensington Gardens

By some miracle of fortune, the 248 hectares of woodland, pasture and lake that make up Hyde Park and Kensington Gardens managed to escape development and have survived as a green lung in the heart of London's West End. Originally a monastic farm, owned by Westminster Abbey, the park was seized by Henry VIII at the Dissolution and turned into a private hunting ground – hence the curious name of **Rotten Row** (a corruption of *Route du Roi*, the 'King's Road'), down which monarchs once rode to hunt deer and today guards from the Household Cavalry Brigade parade on their way to the Changing of the Guard at Buckingham Palace.

An anticlockwise tour of the park will take you west to the **Albert Memorial**, the huge and newly restored monument to Queen Victoria's spouse, the man who organised the Great Exhibition in the park in 1851. On the opposite side of the road is the **Albert Hall**, home to the summer Promenade concerts (the Proms). A path leads northeastwards to the **Serpentine Gallery**, which hosts exhibitions of contemporary

art in summer. The **Serpentine Lake**, with its Lido and swimming pool, was created in 1730 by damming the River Westbourne. Hardy members of the Walrus Club come here to swim daily, even in the depths of winter.

Further north is George Frederick Watt's massive equestrian statue, *Physical Energy* (1904). By way of contrast, the *Peter Pan* (1912) statue commemorates J M Barrie's boyish hero.

The path leads up to Lancaster Gate, then turns right to skirt the northern edge of the park to reach **Speaker's Corner**. Here, on Sunday mornings, soapbox orators address the crowds on subjects dear to their heart. Nearby **Marble Arch** was designed by Nash in 1827, and modelled on Rome's Arch of Constantine, to serve as a triumphant entrance to the grounds of Buckingham Palace until it was moved here in 1851.

Kensington Palace

Kensington Gardens. Tel: (020) 7376 2858; www.hrp.org.uk. Open: daily mid-Mar–mid-Oct, 1000–1700 (last entry), mid-Oct–mid-Mar 1000–1600; closed 24–26 Dec and 1 Jan. ££.

William III, the asthmatic Dutch king who ruled England from 1689 to 1702, created this palace as an escape from London's smog, employing Sir Christopher Wren to design a surprisingly modest Dutch-style country house set in beautiful formal gardens on the edge of Hyde Park. Many of the original 17th-century furnishings have survived, along with William Kent's ceiling paintings executed for George I showing the king, his courtiers and servants in illusionistic detail. Pride of place goes to the sumptuous display of embroidered silk dresses, ostrich-feather fans and velvet shoes that make up the Royal Ceremonial Dress Collection, including dresses designed for the **Queen** by Norman Hartnell and Hardy Amies.

The Natural History Museum

Cromwell Road. Tel: (020) 7938 9123; www.nhm.ac.uk. Open: Mon–Sat 1000–1750, Sun 1100–1750; closed 24, 25, 26 Dec and 1 Jan. ££.

The Natural History Museum is effectively two museums in one, divided into the **Life** and **Earth** galleries, the latter being what used to be the boring old Geology Museum but now transformed into an exciting explanation of the planet we live on. The only problem facing visitors is knowing where to start.

If you have children, the answer is obvious: your young companions will drag you straight off to see the **Dinosaurs**, which are so popular that you may have to queue. You will consider the wait well worth while as you wander among life-size recreations of the giants that stalked the earth millions of years ago, including a clutch of feeding carnivores that look cute enough to take home until they growl menacingly and snap their teeth-laden jaws.

Biology and ecology

If there are simply too many people for comfort among the giant prehistoric reptiles, you could go and check out the **Creepy Crawlies**, which are just as terrifying when blown up from their normal microscopic scale to the size of a sheep or a cat. Teaching your children the facts of life is made painless and embarrassment-free in the **Human Biology** gallery, where helpful pictures and drawings explain how babies are made. From the basics of life to high science, there are videos to explain chromosomes and DNA and hands-on experiments to explain perception, the senses and memory.

Various galleries make good use of the museum's legacy of stuffed animals and pinned butterflies. Nobody today would want to kill animals for display and entertainment, but the museum takes the view that time cannot be reversed so it might as well use its Victorian collections to provide perhaps the only opportunity most visitors will have to come close to a tiger or admire the astonishing beauty of rainforest butterflies and birds.

The restless earth

Do save at least an hour for visiting the **Earth Galleries**, which do an outstanding job of explaining modern geological concepts, such as plate tectonics and volcanic hotspots or plumes that explain why our planet is the way it is today. In case you are tempted to think this unimportant, the displays show how the earth's convection dictates our weather and phenomena such as hurricanes, tidal waves, ice-cap temperature and global warming. And if that all sounds too technical, you can just enjoy the videos, the sound effects and the **Earthquake Experience**, which gives you a taste of how it feels to be caught up in an earthquake in Japan.

Stories in stone

Don't forget to look at the building as you explore the Natural History Museum. The exterior has a terracotta relief running along the entire length of the building depicting animals, fossils and plants (living species to the left of the entrance, extinct ones to the right). The cathedral-like space of the entrance hall was the architect's way of paying homage to God for the multiplicity and beauty of creation – though three years before the museum was designed, Darwin had shattered the Biblical account of Creation with his work The Origin of Species. *Throughout the museum there are playful decorations, from fossil ferns to monkeys scampering up and down the arches.*

The Science Museum

Forget memories of dull school science: the Science Museum is a vast and rambling institution with something for everyone and displays that help you to learn painlessly.

If wood and iron turn you on, along with the imaginary smells of coal and steam, there is the **Power Gallery** (ground floor), devoted to the giants of the Industrial Revolution, where huge Boulton and Watt steam engines attract admiring looks for their gleaming brass and smoothly gliding pistons.

Contrasting with these solid dinosaurs of the engineering world is the astonishingly small and fragile lunar landing module of the adjacent **Exploration of Space Gallery**. If you have ever harboured the desire to be an astronaut, this is the gallery for you, full of insights into the arduous life of space travellers where even simple bodily functions (such as going to the toilet) become complex tasks requiring specialist equipment.

For children

Children are very well catered for. The basement has play areas for toddlers and nursery-school-age children (called the **Garden** and **Things**), whilst older children will find much to amuse them in the gallery called the **Secret Life of the Home**. Ostensibly a history of domestic gadgets from vacuum cleaners to refrigerators, there is much sly humour here, including a microwave oven that opens to reveal a poodle inside and a plastic turd that is endlessly recycled to demonstrate what happens when the lavatory is flushed. Star of the show is the first ever computer game – called Pong, a primitive electronic version of ping-pong – but you won't get near that for the queues of children fighting to have a go.

More serious, but just as much fun, is the **Launch Pad** (first floor) with lots of hands-on experiments to do and learn from. Young gallery attendants perform the vital role of keeping equipment in good working order and explaining the scientific principles being demonstrated. The brief lectures that are given throughout the day in the adjacent theatre are well worth attending.

An oasis of calm

If children and noise appal you, don't worry: there is a secret refuge on the top floor devoted to the **Science and Art of Medicine**. Children rarely penetrate to spoil your concentration as you wander through a maze of exhibits, ranging from fascinating archaeological material from ancient Egypt, Greece and Rome to gruesomely realistic wax anatomical models.

Other highlights include the **On Air** gallery (third floor), which lets you make and broadcast your own radio programme, or use a computer to mix your own hit record; the nearby **Flight Gallery** allows you to sit at the controls of a Cessna 150 light aircraft, or try flying a helicopter; and the **Food for Thought Gallery** (first floor) shows how our diet has changed over the last 100 years and offers some dietary hints for living to a ripe old age.

Getting there: Exhibition Road. Tel: (020) 7942 4454; www.nmsi.ac.uk. Open: daily 1000–1800; closed 24, 25, 26 Dec and 1 Jan. ££.

New for the Millennium

In the last five years or so, the sheer speed of technological change has left many of the exhibits at the Science Museum looking antiquated and out of date in content and presentation style. There is little on the digital revolution, the Internet, Quantum physics or relativity. All this should change in June 2000 with the opening of the new gallery entitled The Making of the Modern World, adding one-third more space to this already vast museum.

The Victoria and Albert Museum

South Kensington. Tel: (020) 7938 8500; www.vam.ac.uk. Open: daily 1000–1745 (to 2130 on Wed in summer and main holiday periods); closed 24, 25, 26 Dec and 1 Jan. ££ (free after 1630).

The V&A describes itself as 'The National Museum of Art and Design', which is as close as anyone could probably get to summing up the scale and range of the contents, which include (just to name a few highlights) a comprehensive display of **dress and fashion** through the ages (the museum also hosts fashion shows, on occasions, that are open to all comers); a vast collection of **glass**, from the earliest Egyptian perfume jars to modern avant-garde creations; **textiles** from all over the world, including richly coloured cottons and silks from India and intricately decorated kimonos from Japan; and pioneering examples of **20th-century design**, from Zanussi fridges to Dyson vacuum cleaners.

Highlights and contrasts

And that is just the tip of the iceberg – there are 145 galleries altogether in what is indisputably the **world's largest museum devoted to applied design**. One way to experience the collection is just to drift and experience the contrasts. You might stumble across the **Great Bed of Ware**, 10 ft wide and 13 ft long, elaborately carved around 1590 and mentioned in the plays of Shakespeare and Ben Jonson. Or you could end up in the cast room, face to face with casts and copies of the great antique and Renaissance sculptures. You might find your curiosity stimulated by the model of the tiger in the Nehru Gallery of **Indian Art** which is depicted in the act of eating a British Army officer (a small organ inside the tiger imitates the groans of the dying victim, but sadly it is rarely played). Or you might discover one of the V&A's great secrets: the large collection of great art that is hung in the Henry Cole wing, where paintings by **John Constable** compete for attention with bronzes by **Degas** and the architectural drawings of **Frank Lloyd Wright**, not to mention the rooftop views to be had from the windows of the upper floors.

The V&A has some innovative schemes that might enrich your social life: Wednesday evening **Late Views**, with drinks and live music (plus candle-lit restaurant), are a great way to meet potential soul mates and the weekend and school holiday **activities** are excellent for keeping bright children entertained while you go and enjoy **brunch** with live jazz in the basement café (Sun only).

New for the Millennium

Controversially, the museum plans to build an innovative and ultra-modern extension, called **the Spiral** and designed by Daniel Libeskind, due to open in 2004 (critics don't despise the design, they just think that it's in the wrong place and that it will fight horribly with the eclectic Victorian style of neighbouring buildings – judge for yourself by visiting the displays in the museum entrance).

Honour to the founder

The V&A was founded in 1852 to support and encourage excellence in design and to continue the work of the Great Exhibition of 1851, a celebration of the arts, crafts and industrial products of the British Empire. The driving force behind both was ***Prince Albert****, a far-sighted genius who recognised the critical importance of design and technology to future economic prosperity.*

Shopping

Knightsbridge has some of London's best up-market shopping. As well as the big department stores, there are scores of classy designer outlets and small specialist shops in Beauchamp Place, Brompton Road, Sloane Street and the King's Road, so it pays just to walk and look around.

General Trading Co

144 Sloane Street. Tel: (020) 7730 0411. Set in four rambling houses just off Sloane Square, this store sells oriental and exotic home furnishings from Balinese carved fruits and Thai silks to Vietnamese lacquer bowls.

Harrods

87–135 Brompton Road. Tel: (020) 7730 1234. One of the world's best-known stores is worth a visit for the wonderful **art-deco food halls** alone. Famous for selling just about anything, the store has a full programme of events, author signings and product demonstrations.

Harvey Nichols

109–123 Knightsbridge. Tel: (020) 7235 5000. Designer label clothing, furnishings and accessories, crowned by a foodies paradise on the top floor.

Peter Jones

Sloane Square. Tel: (020) 7730 8886. Low-key department store that doesn't advertise or flaunt fashionable credentials, but stocks all your household needs, specialising in quality furnishings and domestic goods at competitive prices.

Portobello Road Market

Portobello Road. One of London's best markets, as much for the shops in the surrounding streets as for the stalls. The general market (food, clothing, records, and books) operates Monday to Saturday and is supplemented by a huge antiques market on Sat, clothes and bric-à-brac on Fri, Sat and Sun and organic food on Thur.

Nightlife

Royal Albert Hall

Kensington Gore. Tel: (020) 7589 8212. Massive domed concert hall with an eclectic mix of events from wrestling and rock to the famous **Promenade concerts**. Events are advertised in weekend newspapers such as the *Sunday Times*.

Royal Court

Sloane Square. Tel: (020) 7565 5050. A theatre with a reputation for experimental drama by young playwrights – some of whom go on to make it big.

Eating and drinking

There are few bargains to be had in the Knightsbridge and Kensington area – this is moneyed territory – but there are some seriously good restaurants for those prepared to splash out on a special occasion.

Bibendum Oyster Bar

Michelin House, 81 Fulham Road. Tel: (020) 7823 7925. Bookings not accepted. £££. Combine shopping at the next-door **Conran Shop**, home of cutting-edge interior design, with lunch at this informal restaurant set in the former Michelin building and decorated with art-deco tile work. Push the boat out with a seafood platter or caviar, or snack on oysters, crayfish or crab. The restaurant in the same building (*tel: (020) 7581 58171; booking essential*) works miracles with humble peasant dishes from around the world (from Basque ham and beans to the UK's own fish and chips).

Chelsea Kitchen

98 King's Road. Tel: (020) 7589 1330. £.

Stockpot

273 King's Road. Tel: (020) 7823 3175. £. Two branches of the same chain selling filling and wholesome food at rock-bottom prices. Vegetarian options. Crowded but fun.

Harrods' Famous Deli

Harrods Ground Floor, Knightsbridge. Tel: (020) 7730 1234, ext 2997. ££. New Yorkers hungry for soul food should head here for classic salt beef or pastrami on rye, or blueberry cheesecake. Sit-down and takeaway service.

Pizza on the Park

11 Knightsbridge. Tel: (020) 7235 5273. ££. The flagship restaurant in this up-market pizza chain is renowned as much for the quality of the **jazz** (you never know who might turn up for a session) as for the authenticity of its pizzas. Great atmosphere.

Star Tavern

6 Belgrave Mews West. Tel: (020) 7234 2806. £. Time stands still at this old-fashioned pub, with warming fires, antique furnishings, club-like atmosphere and traditional pub meals (*Mon to Fri only*).

The Fifth Floor

Harvey Nichols, Knightsbridge. Café tel: (020) 7823 1839. ££. Restaurant tel: (020) 7235 5250. £££. Choose from the café, popular with shopaholics and serving tantalisingly tasty snacks, or the restaurant, which is strictly for those who don't mind spending serious money. Both serve quality ingredients combined with eclectic flair.

Vong

The Berkeley Hotel, Wilton Place. Tel: (020) 7235 1010. £££. **Vietnamese** with flair. There is nowhere else in London where you can enjoy the melting magic of crab spring rolls, tender soya-roast quail or lobster *daikon*. Not cheap but worth every penny.

Chelsea

Chelsea is a place where people go to see and be seen – a great place for watching people in all their eccentric variety. Bohemian sensibilities are the norm in a 'village' that has more than its fair share of actors and artists, writers and style pundits.

Chelsea's self-image is best summed up in the type of MP that it elects to parliament: the late **Alan Clark**, the wittily acerbic war historian, diarist, adulterer and apologist for Margaret Thatcher and more recently **Michael Portillo**, the sexually liberated, Spanish émigré, child actor, would-be Tory leader – and apologist for **Margaret Thatcher**. Yes, that's right – no matter how artistic the sensibilities of the average Chelsea-ite, they are true blue to the core, a bastion of conservative political values based on their desire to protect their immense wealth and accumulate more.

The wealth is not visible to anyone walking down the rather tacky **King's Road**, Chelsea's High Street. To find the wealth you have to wander through Cadogan Square or Pont Street

to admire the blocks of perfect Arts-and-Crafts and Queen-Anne-style houses that lie to the north, between the King's Road and Knightsbridge, or head south to Chelsea Embankment and see Cheyne Walk and Tite Street, home at various dates to **Dante Gabriel Rossetti**, **Oscar Wilde** and **Mick Jagger**.

One house in Cheyne Row (*No 24*) can be visited: **Carlyle's House**, home of the great 19th-century polemicist, is owned by the National Trust (*Infoline: tel: (01494) 755559; open: Easter–end Oct, Wed–Sat, 1100–1700; ££*) and offers a glimpse of the world that lies behind Chelsea's elegant façades.

Beautifully tended gardens are a defining feature of Chelsea houses: Carlyle's House has one (it was the only place the great man was allowed to smoke since Jane, his wife, couldn't stand the smell) but the doyen of them all is the **Chelsea Physic Garden** (*66 Royal Hospital Road; open: Easter–end Oct, Wed 1200–1700 and Sun 1400–1800; ££*), so called because it was founded by apothecaries in 1673 as a place for research into herbal medicine.

The best time to see this richly planted garden is during **Chelsea Festival Week** (*21–25 June*) or after a visit to the **Chelsea Flower Show** (*24–28 May*), which is as much a social event as a celebration of matters horticultural. The Flower Show is held in the grounds of the **Chelsea Royal Hospital** (*tel: (020) 7730 0161; open: daily except Sun, 1000–1600; ££*), which can be visited throughout the year for Sir Christopher Wren's splendid buildings, Grinling Gibbons's carved wooden choir-stalls and its portraits of Charles I (by Van Dyck), Charles II (by Lely) and James II (by Kneller).

Westminster, Whitehall and St James's

Edward the Confessor moved the royal court out of the City in 1042. Ever since, Westminster has been London's political and religious power base and the symbolic heart of Britain's democratic system. Nearby St James's has some of London's oldest and most exclusive shops.

BEST OF

Westminster, Whitehall and St James's

*Getting there: the most useful **underground** stations are Westminster and St James's Park, though Victoria and Charing Cross are also close, and both Piccadilly Circus and Green Park are convenient for St James's. Westminster Pier is served by frequent **riverboat** services from Greenwich and the Tower of London.*

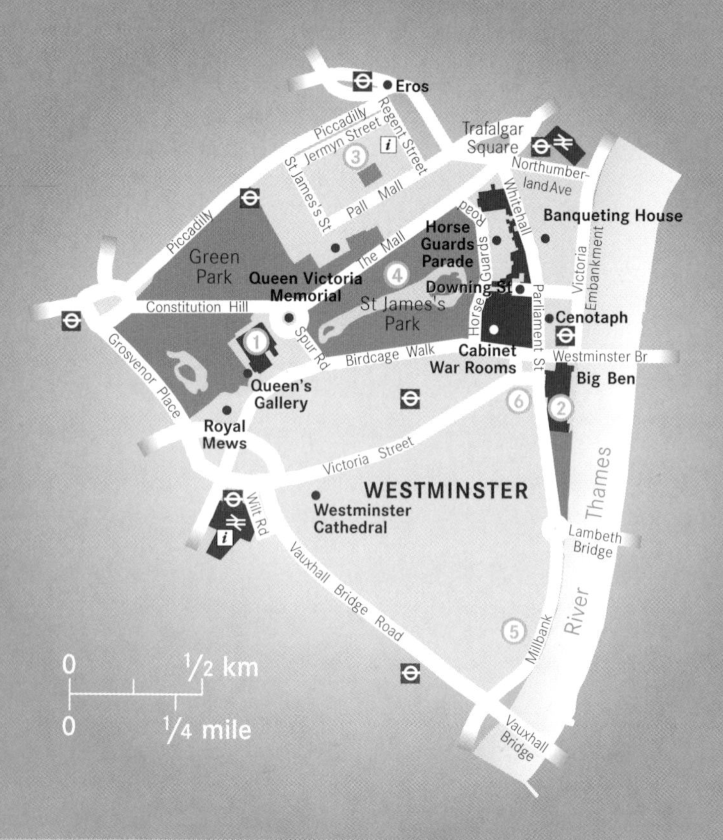

① *Buckingham Palace*

It may only be open to the public for a few weeks each summer, but the Queen's London residence attracts hordes of visitors every day, hoping for a glimpse of the royals or drawn by the pageantry of the Changing of the Guard. **Pages 40–1**

② *Houses of Parliament*

This Victorian Gothic masterpiece is the defining feature of the London landscape, best seen at night from across the River Thames. Join the queues outside if you want to hear a debate, but don't expect the chamber to be full. **Pages 44–5**

③ *Jermyn Street*

If you know any men with a taste for cigars, port and handmade shirts seek out this street of old-fashioned shops, patronised by the Royal Family and the wealthy bachelors who frequent the gentlemen's clubs of St James's.
Page 50

④ *St James's Park*

This pretty, willow-fringed and duck-filled park makes a peaceful retreat from the bustle of the city. It has footpaths, a lake and splendid views of Buckingham Palace and the government buildings of Whitehall.
Page 46

⑤ *Tate Britain*

The national collection of British art is the only major gallery in London to be devoted exclusively to British artists, covering the full spectrum from the 16th century to the present day.
Page 47

⑥ *Westminster Abbey*

The burial place of statesmen and poets and the place where kings and queens are crowned, this church has been at the heart of the nation's political and religious life for almost a thousand years.
Pages 48–9

Tip

Go during the week if you want to see Parliament in session, go at weekends for peace and quiet.

Banqueting House

Whitehall. Underground: Westminster or Charing Cross. Tel: (020) 7930 4179. Open: Mon–Sat 1000–1700; closed on Bank Holidays and 24 Dec–1 Jan. Closed at short notice for government functions. £.

Completed in 1622, the Banqueting House is the only remaining part of the old Whitehall Palace, the principal royal residence in London, which was destroyed by a fire in 1689. It was commissioned by **James I** after an earlier fire; the architect Inigo Jones, who had travelled widely in Italy, used the opportunity to introduce the classical ideals of the Italian Renaissance to Britain. The ceiling paintings, by the Flemish master **Rubens**, were commissioned by **Charles I** in 1629 to commemorate his father, James I, who as King of both England and Scotland was proclaimed King of Great Britain in 1604. It was from this very room that Charles I stepped out onto the scaffold for his execution in 1649, following his defeat in the **English Civil War**

Buckingham Palace

At the end of The Mall by St James's Park. Tel: (020) 7321 2233; www.royal.gov.uk. Underground: Green Park or Victoria. Open: Aug–Sept, 0930–1630 daily. £££. Credit card bookings available by telephone.

Buckingham Palace has been the official London residence of the monarch since **Queen Victoria** moved here on her accession in 1837. The present building, popularly known as Buck House, was largely designed in the 1820s by the Regency architect **John Nash** and takes its name from its former use as the London home of the Duke of Buckingham. The east front, the public face of the palace from The Mall, was added in 1912. The Royal Standard flies from the flagpole on the east front, whenever the Queen is in residence.

> “*They're changing guard at Buckingham Palace*
> *Christopher Robin went down with Alice*
> *We looked for the King, but he never came*
> *'Well, God take care of him, all the same,'*
> *Says Alice.*”

A A Milne, *When We Were Very Young*, 1924

Since 1993 it has been possible to visit the palace during those few weeks each summer when the royal court moves to **Balmoral** in Scotland.

The tour takes in a succession of sumptuous rooms, including the State Dining Room and the Throne Room. The highlight is Nash's vaulted Picture Gallery, which stretches down the centre of the palace and contains masterpieces from the Royal Collection by **Rubens**, **Rembrandt**, **Van Dyck** and others.

The monarchy has been criticised for lack of access to the collection and the **Queen's Gallery** is currently undergoing a major refurbishment, so that more exhibition space will be available for changing displays. It will reopen in spring 2002 to mark the Queen's Golden Jubilee. In the meantime, you can still visit the **Royal Mews** (*entrance on Buckingham Palace Road; open: Mon–Thur 1200–1600; ££*), where the gilded state carriages are kept, along with liveried horses in working stables. The star attraction here is the Gold Carriage, made for George III in 1762, and used at coronations.

The ceremony of the **Changing of the Guard**, in which soldiers from the Queen's regiments formally hand over the keys to the palace, takes place in the forecourt on alternate mornings at 1130 (*daily between April and July*). The mounted sentries, in their scarlet tunics and bearskin caps, make a colourful sight and the ceremony is extremely popular, so arrive early if you want a prime position by the railings.

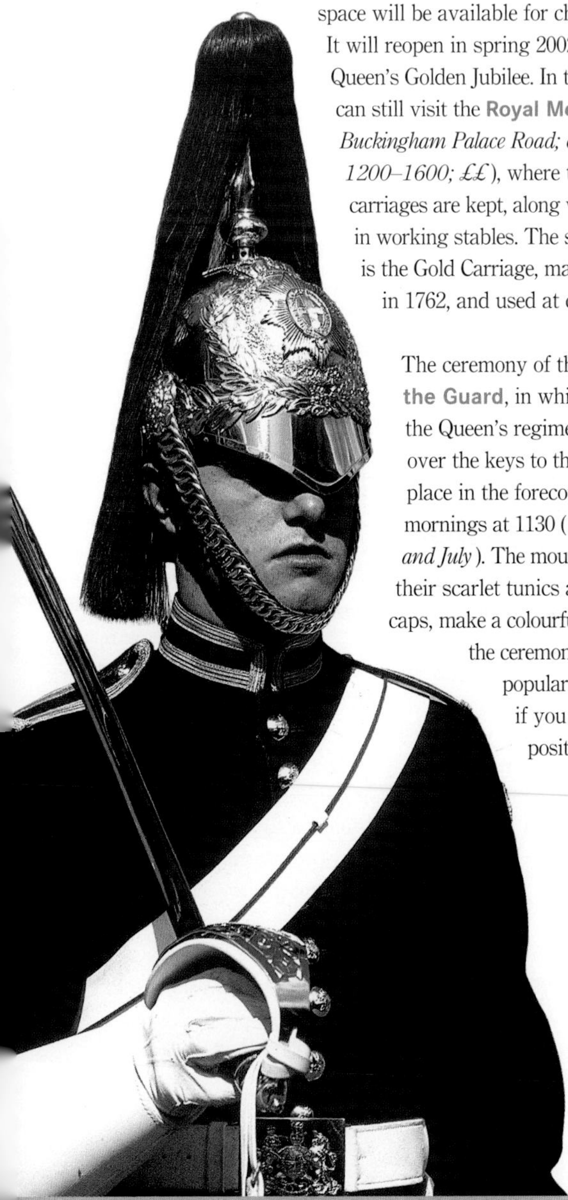

Cabinet War Rooms

Clive Steps, King Charles Street. Tel: (020) 7930 6961; www.iwm.org.uk. Underground: Westminster or St James's Park. Open: 1000–1800 daily. ££ (children free).

Step through a sandbagged doorway behind the Foreign Office and you enter a warren of underground rooms that served as the nerve centre of British operations during the Second World War. This concrete and steel-reinforced bunker is where **Winston Churchill** and his ministers slept, ate and planned the military campaign against Germany, safe from the bombing raids which were taking place overhead. Everything has been left exactly as it was in 1945, giving a fascinating, almost nostalgic insight into wartime conditions. On the self-guided audio tour, which takes about an hour, you can listen to eyewitness accounts of the war and peek into rooms such as the Map Room, Cabinet Room and Churchill's bedroom, where he spent many hours sitting up in bed, working and smoking cigars. Another room, disguised even to staff as the Prime Minister's private toilet, was actually a secret telephone link with a hotline to **The White House**. Among the items on display is the map on which Churchill and others carved up Europe in the post-war settlement agreed at Yalta between the Allies and the USSR, thus laying the foundations of the long Cold War which followed.

> *“Grey city*
> *Stubbornly implanted*
> *Taken so for granted*
> *For a thousand years*
> *Stay, city,*
> *Smokily enchanted*
> *Cradle of our memories*
> *and hopes and fears.”*

Noel Coward (1889–1973), *London Pride*, the song which epitomised London's wartime resistance

Downing Street and Whitehall

Underground: Westminster or Charing Cross.

The names of these two London streets have become so familiar that they are now virtually synonymous with what they represent – on the news, 'Downing Street' is used to refer to the Prime Minister and 'Whitehall' to top civil servants. The house at No 10 Downing Street was built in the 1680s and was given by the king to Britain's first prime minister, **Sir Robert Walpole**, in 1732. Since then it has always been the official residence of the British premier, though the present incumbent, **Tony Blair**, lives at No 11, the residence of the Chancellor of the Exchequer, where there is more room for his young family. Downing Street has been closed to the public since 1990, when the then prime minister, **Margaret Thatcher**, had protective iron railings installed – not enough to prevent a terrorist bomb exploding in the garden of No 10 the following year.

Whitehall has traditionally been home to the major government ministries; the 'big two', the **Foreign Office** and **Treasury**, face each other across King Charles Street. On Whitehall itself, the main focus of attention is the **Cenotaph**, a simple monument designed by **Sir Edwin Lutyens** in 1920 and now the national memorial to the dead of the two world wars. It is here that the Queen and leading members of the government lay wreaths on Remembrance Sunday each November. Further up Whitehall, **Horse Guards** is a three-sided building whose archway serves as the official entrance to the royal palaces. During the day, the building is guarded by mounted troopers of the Life Guards and Blues and Royals. The guard is changed at 1100 each morning (1000 on Sunday) in a ceremony that is generally less crowded than its equivalent at Buckingham Palace.

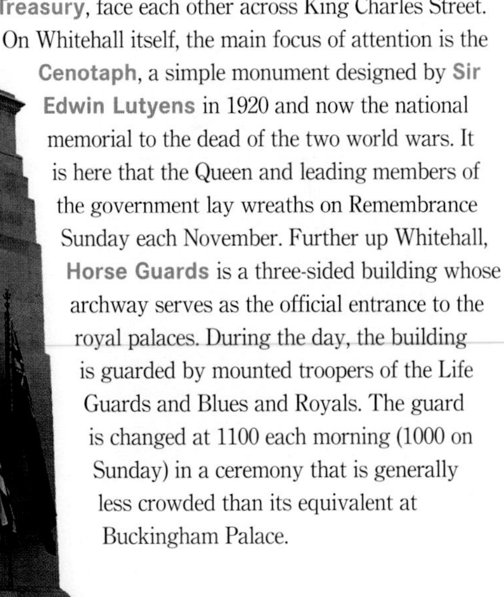

Houses of Parliament

The home of the 'Mother of Parliaments' is among the best-known and best-loved of all London landmarks, its long riverfront façade the capital's most photographed sight.

The first palace was built here in the 11th century by **Edward the Confessor** and it remained the chief royal residence until **Henry VIII** moved the court to Whitehall. **Guy Fawkes** tried to blow up the building in 1605 (an event still commemorated across Britain with bonfires each 5 November) and it was finally destroyed by fire in 1834. **Charles Barry** and **Augustus Pugin** produced the Victorian Gothic masterpiece that stands today, a riot of pinnacles, towers and medieval tracery in honey-coloured limestone which reflects the sunlight off the River Thames. Prominent in the view is the Westminster Clock Tower, otherwise known as **Big Ben** after its giant bell, the most famous symbol of the Houses of Parliament, whose chimes are heard around the world via the BBC.

Parliament is divided into two chambers. The **House of Commons** is made up of elected Members of Parliament (MPs), while the **House of Lords** now consists largely of working peers appointed by the government, its traditional hereditary element of titled landowners having been abolished in 1999. When either house is sitting, it is possible to attend debates, though you may have to queue for at least an hour. The longest queues are usually for the House of Commons. British citizens can write to their MP requesting tickets for **Question Time**, which takes place on weekday afternoons, with the Prime Minister answering questions on Wednesdays. Your MP may also be able to arrange a guided tour. Otherwise, join the queue outside St Stephen's Entrance for admission to the Strangers' Gallery, from where the public is allowed to view proceedings. From Monday to Wednesday, the House sits until at least 2200 and it is generally easier to get in after 1800.

As you enter the building, look down to the left to see **Westminster Hall**, the only surviving part of the 11th-century Palace of Westminster; its magnificent hammerbeam roof was completed in 1402. Continue into **St Stephen's Hall**, on the site of an old chapel where the medieval parliamentarians faced one another across the choir-stalls. This is the origin of the adversarial shape of the Commons chamber, with government and opposition benches separated by a distance equivalent to the length of two swords. Proceedings in the House of Lords are overseen by the Lord Chancellor, who sits astride a cushion known as the **Woolsack**. Each year, the **Queen** makes a speech to Parliament in the House of Lords, but no monarch has been allowed in the Commons since Charles I attempted to arrest five MPs in 1642. All of this is explained in an exhibition at the **Jewel Tower** (*open: 1000–1800 daily in summer, 1000–1600 in winter; £*), the 14th-century fortress across the road.

“And after our lovers had come under Charing Cross Bridge the Houses of Parliament rose before them at the end of a great crescent of golden lamps, blue and faint, halfway between the earth and sky. And the clock on the Tower was like a November sun.”

H G Wells, *Love and Mr Lewisham*, 1900

Getting there: Westminster. Tel: (020) 7219 4272; www.parliament.uk. Underground: Westminster. Open when Parliament is sitting, generally Mon–Wed from 1430, Thur 1130 and Fri 0930, but closed during the summer recess from Aug–Oct.

St James's Park

Underground: St James's Park.

The green space which links Downing Street to Buckingham Palace is the prettiest and most intimate of all London's royal parks. From the bridge across the lake there are unbroken views of Buckingham Palace in one direction and the domes and turrets of Whitehall in the other. Office workers come here in summer with their picnic lunches to escape the noise and bustle of the city, but at times the park can be too crowded for its own good, the peace disturbed by the chatter of mobile phones.

The Mall, which runs alongside the park, is a processional route linking Buckingham Palace to Trafalgar Square. Beyond The Mall, **St James's Palace** is a 16th-century red-brick Tudor palace which was the official royal residence from 1698 to 1837. The **Prince of Wales** has a home here and the **Queen Mother** lives in neighbouring Clarence House. The only part of St James's Palace open to the public is the Chapel Royal, scene of a number of royal weddings including that of Queen Victoria. Between October and Easter, services are held here on Sundays at 11.15; from Easter to July, they move to the Queen's Chapel across the road. St James's Palace stands near the start of **Pall Mall**, London's first-ever gaslit street, which takes its name from the curious game of pell mell, an early form of croquet which Charles II used to play here. The street is best known as the home of London's most traditional gentlemen's clubs, such as the Athenaeum and the Reform.

Tate Britain

Millbank. Tel: (020) 7887 8000; www.tate.org.uk. Underground: Pimlico. Open: daily 1000–1750; closed 24–26 Dec and 1 Jan. Free.

Established in 1897 by the sugar magnate **Henry Tate**, who donated his own collection to found a national gallery of British art, the Tate Gallery has long outgrown its original purpose and building. As a result the collection has been split in two, with international art being displayed at **Tate Modern** (*see page 132*) and British art (from the 16th century to the present) being displayed here, at Tate Britain, in a series of new galleries, some of which are already open, while the rest are scheduled for completion in May 2001.

> *"It is difficult to speak adequately or justly of London. It is not a pleasant place; it is not agreeable, or cheerful, or easy, or exempt from reproach. It is only magnificent."*
>
> **Henry James (1843–1916)**

The collection spans the full range of British styles, from the portraits of **William Hogarth** to the landscapes of **John Constable** and the great pre-Raphaelite painters **Millais**, **Rossetti** and **Holman Hunt**. Among particular works to look out for are Constable's *Flatford Mill*, Millais' *Ophelia* and William Frith's *Derby Day*, with its vivid portrayals of swindlers, toffs and gypsies. Works are arranged thematically and frequently rotated, and even in the new galleries it will not be possible to show the entire collection, so a good start is to take one of the regular free guided tours (for details, check at the information desk in the rotunda).

An annexe, the Clore Gallery, opened in 1987, houses some 20,000 items bequeathed by **J M W Turner**, England's greatest landscape painter. Among the items on permanent display are Turner's scenes of Venice and Rome and pastoral landscapes painted in the Thames Valley.

Westminster Abbey

Broad Sanctuary. Tel: (020) 7222 5152; www.westminster-abbey.org.uk. Underground: Westminster or St James's Park. Open: Mon–Fri 0930–1545 (late opening 1800–1945 Wed); Sat 0900–1345; closed 24–26 Dec and 1 Jan. Closed on Sundays except for services (admission free). ££.

With its memorials and monuments to statesmen, soldiers and kings, Westminster Abbey can seem more like an enormous mausoleum or funereal theme park than a living church. Crowds of tourists throng the aisles and it is difficult to experience anything approaching a sense of spirituality or peace. Yet a visit here is essential if you are to understand English history and the part that this church has played in public life for almost a thousand years.

It was founded in the 11th century by **Edward the Confessor**, when he moved the royal court out of the City to 'west minster', the church in the west. Edward died a week after the abbey's consecration on 28 December 1065 and became the first monarch to be buried here. A year later, **William the Conqueror** was crowned in Westminster Abbey, beginning a tradition that has continued with just two exceptions to this day. The present church was rebuilt in French Gothic style by **Henry II** in 1245, though the most spectacular section of all, the **Lady Chapel**, was added by **Henry VII** in the 16th century.

Visitors enter through the north transept, otherwise known as Statesmen's Aisle, where former prime ministers, among them **Gladstone** and **Pitt the Elder**, are buried.

Turn left to reach Henry VII's chapel, filled with royal tombs including **Elizabeth I, Mary, Queen of Scots** and Henry VII himself. Take time to look up and admire the magnificent fan-vaulted ceiling. Near here, at the heart of the abbey, is the shrine of St Edward the Confessor, the abbey's founder. His tomb is found close to the **Coronation Chair** where kings and queens are crowned.

The rest of the abbey is a tribute to the great and good of British history. **Poets' Corner** contains monuments to **Chaucer**, **Shakespeare**, **Dickens**, **Dr Johnson**, **Thomas Hardy** and **D H Lawrence. Musicians' Aisle** features memorials to **Elgar**, **Vaughan Williams**, **Benjamin Britten** and **Henry Purcell**, who was organist here. The explorer **David Livingstone**, the naturalist **Charles Darwin** and the statesman **Clement Attlee** are all buried in the nave, where there is also a memorial stone to **Winston Churchill**.

Most poignant of all is the **Tomb of the Unknown Warrior**, 'unknown by name or rank, brought from France to lie among the most illustrious in the land' and buried with military honours on Remembrance Day 1920. The tomb stands in silent tribute to more than one million British soldiers who gave their lives during the First World War.

Westminster Cathedral

Victoria Street. Underground: Victoria. Tel: (020) 7798 9055.
Open: 0700–1900 daily. Free.

This Byzantine-style cathedral, begun in 1895, is the seat of the Archbishop of Westminster, head of the **Roman Catholic Church** in Britain. The cathedral has never been completed, leading to a curious effect, as if man in his vanity had covered the lower levels with marble and mosaic and God in his wisdom had decided to leave the upper levels bare. The peaceful church stands in stark contrast to its surroundings, among the noisy, traffic-choked streets of Victoria. From the viewing gallery in the bell tower there are panoramic views of London.

Shopping

Many of the shops in St James's date back to the 18th century. With their poky interiors and dark wood panelling, they cultivate an image of old-fashioned exclusivity.

The main shopping street, called Jermyn Street, is almost entirely devoted to tailors and shops for the man about town. Beginning at the Haymarket end, you soon arrive at **Herbie Frogg** (*No 18*), which sells shirts, suits and ties of modern cut. In the same stretch is **Geo F Trumper** (*No 20*), a gentlemen's barber and perfumer, and **Bates the Hatter** (*No 21A*), purveyors of top hats, trilbies, fedoras and panamas. **Church's** (*No 110*) sells solid English shoes, while **Harvie & Hudson** (*Nos 77 and 97*) is a bespoke tailor and shirtmaker whose range includes silk dressing gowns, cummerbunds, cashmere overcoats, braces and velvet slippers. Orders take several weeks and the minimum order is four shirts, but there are always ready-to-wear items in stock.

The Prince of Wales buys his shirts at **Turnbull & Asser** (*No 71*) and his toiletries at **Floris** (*No 89*), established in 1730 and proudly known as the Queen's perfumers. For something different, don't miss **Paxton & Whitfield** (*No 93*), the cheesemongers that supplies the royal households. It's worth going in just to smell the cheeses; they also sell hams, pork pies and fine wines.

St James's Street

Best known for its gentlemen's clubs, hidden behind discreet, nameless brass plaques, St James's Street also has its share of old-fashioned shops. At the lower end of the street, look out for **Berry Bros & Rudd** (*No 3*), London's oldest wine merchant, as well as **Lock & Co** (*No 6*), makers of hats since 1676. The bowler hat was invented here and past customers have included Lord Nelson and the Duke of Wellington. **Lobb** (*No 7*) produces handmade boots and shoes for the Royal Family. **James J Fox** (*No 19*) sells cigars, pipes, tobacco and snuff and **D R Harris** (*No 29*) is an 18th-century chemist's shop. Across the street, **William Evans** (*No 67A*) specialises in guns, hunting and fishing gear, **Hugh Johnson** (*No 68*) is a well-known Master of Wine and **Truefitt & Hill** (*No 71*), Prince Philip's barbers, offer a luxury shaving and grooming service as well as gifts such as shaving brushes.

Restaurants and pubs

Che

23 St James's Street. Tel: (020) 7747 9380. £££. This trendy restaurant and cigar bar, named after a Cuban revolutionary, is situated in the heart of stuffy, capitalist St James's. The cigar bar downstairs has a wall-length humidor, while the restaurant features modern European cooking in a bright, airy space.

Red Lion

23 Crown Passage. Tel: (020) 7930 4141. £. One of London's oldest 'village pubs' is found down a cobbled passage between King Street and Pall Mall. The atmosphere is olde-worlde, the beer is good and the food is standard pub grub such as soup, sandwiches and steak pie.

Red Lion

48 Parliament Street. Tel: (020) 7930 5826. £. This popular Whitehall pub is where politicians gather in the evenings. A TV monitor broadcasts live parliamentary debates and a division bell summons MPs to the House of Commons, with plenty of time to race across the road to take part in crucial votes.

Wiltons

55 Jermyn Street. Tel: (020) 7629 9955. £££. This very traditional English restaurant, in keeping with its surroundings, specialises in oysters, fresh fish and game in season. Men are expected to wear a jacket and tie and jeans are not allowed.

Christie's

Even if you can't afford to buy, drop into Christie's *(*8 King St*) to get a feel for the atmosphere of a London auction house. There are always items on view and you can look through the catalogues for forthcoming exhibitions, but if possible, try and go to a sale. Thousands of pounds change hands every minute and in 1989 a Van Gogh painting sold here for £25 million. A word of warning – don't catch the auctioneer's eye, and unless you are extremely rich, never be tempted to bid unless you have planned it carefully in advance.*

St John's, Smith Square

This converted baroque church is a popular setting for lunchtime and evening concerts, many broadcast live on BBC radio. It is situated on the same square as the Conservative Party's head office in an area of Westminster where a number of MPs have their homes. Tel: (020) 7222 1061.

River trips

'Many Londoners live out their lives without ever comprehending the most significant thing about London, that it is a port, a great port', wrote R J Cruikshank in 1951 in his book The Moods of London.

The River Thames is the lifeblood of the city and a cruise on the river an essential London experience. The most popular departure point is **Westminster Pier**, beneath Westminster Bridge on the north bank (others are at Embankment and Greenwich). The variety of tours on offer include circular cruises, lunchtime and dinner cruises, showboat cruises and simple sightseeing boats, with an entertaining commentary provided. For evening cruises it is worth booking in advance, but for most others, except during the peak summer season, you can just turn up and buy a ticket at one of the ticket booths beside the pier.

Upriver cruises, for which you need to allow a full day, make the journey from Westminster to Hampton Court between March and October. This is a beautiful ride into the semi-rural outskirts of London, passing Chelsea, Battersea, Putney, Richmond and Kingston, with their riverside pubs and parks. **Down river**, there are regular cruises throughout the year

from Westminster and Embankment to the Tower of London and Greenwich. Some of the cruises continue past the Millennium Dome to the Thames Flood Barrier at Woolwich, a series of ten movable gates built in 1984 to prevent London from flooding. Here, with seagulls swooping over tidal flats, you begin to appreciate that London is a city by the sea.

There are other options beside pleasure boats. As London's traffic gridlock increases, the river is returning to use as a valuable **public transport** resource. Fast commuter ferries connect Embankment with Bankside, London Bridge City and Canary Wharf for a single, flat fare. Another ferry covers the 'Pool of London', linking attractions on the north and south banks around Tower Bridge. During 2000, a new millennium route will link the London Eye near County Hall by river with the Millennium Dome and from 2001 there should be a riverbus connection between the Tate galleries at Millbank and Bankside.

> “*Earth has not anything to show more fair*
> *Dull would he be of soul who could pass by*
> *A sight so touching in its majesty ...* ”

William Wordsworth,
***Composed Upon Westminster Bridge*, 1802**

Mayfair and Marylebone

Here are London's principal shopping streets – Oxford Street, Regent Street and Piccadilly – while to the north is one of London's finest parks.

BEST OF

Mayfair and Marylebone

Getting there: for Mayfair, the most useful ***underground*** *stations are Bond Street, Green Park, Marble Arch, Oxford Circus and Piccadilly Circus. For Marylebone, the best are Baker Street, Great Portland Street, Oxford Circus and Regent's Park. Oxford Circus, at the junction of Oxford Street and Regent Street, makes a good starting point for both districts as it is on three underground lines and most attractions are a short walk away.*

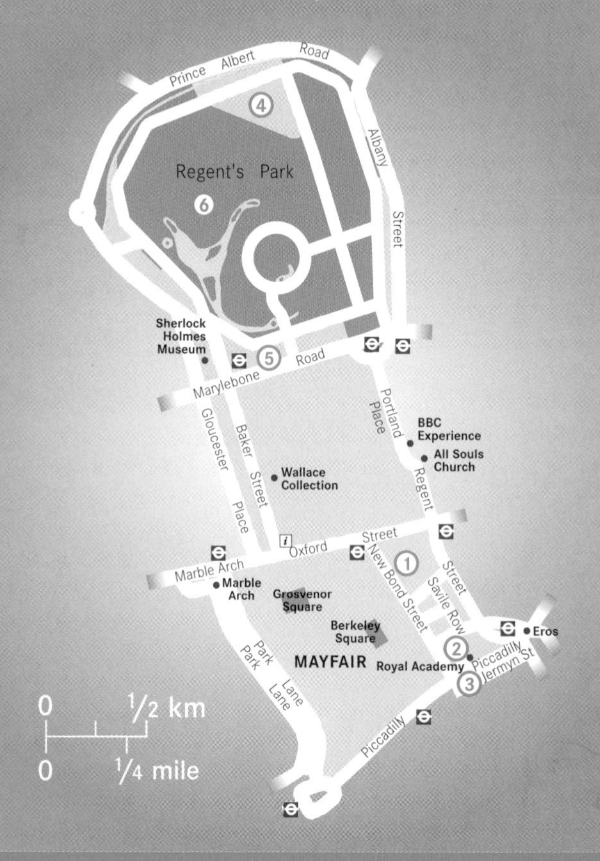

① Bond Street

London's most fashionable shopping street is where old money meets new and tradition comes face to face with cutting-edge design. Don't worry about the lack of price tags – if you need to ask, you probably can't afford it.
Pages 58–9

② Burlington Arcade

This splendid Regency shopping arcade is still patrolled by uniformed 'beadles' who enforce the rules against singing and whistling. A great place for window-shopping, but don't go into the shops unless you have an appointment or a high credit card limit. Page 59

③ Fortnum & Mason

London's top grocer's shop was established in 1707 and continues to supply the leading tables of the capital. A Fortnum's hamper, full of cheeses, chocolates and fine wines, is the perfect gift with which to impress your food-loving friends. Page 66

④ London Zoo

This was the first zoo in the world when it opened in 1828 and visitors still flock here to see the elephants, lions and penguins. The latest attraction is a new exhibition on the theme of biodiversity.
Pages 60–1

⑤ Madame Tussaud's

Kitschy it may be, crowded it certainly is, but unlike its many imitators this is the real thing. The waxworks, founded by Madame Tussaud after the French Revolution, is still the best place in London to see the famous and the infamous throughout history.
Pages 62–3

⑥ Regent's Park

This pleasant mix of landscaped gardens, greensward, fountains, statues and lakes is surrounded by handsome Regency architecture and makes a delightful place to stroll at any time of year. Page 61

Tip

Unwind from your shopping with a stroll around Mayfair's squares, such as Berkeley Square and Grosvenor Square, or relax with a picnic in Mount Street Gardens, one of London's loveliest and least-known parks.

BBC Experience

Broadcasting House, Portland Place. Advance bookings: 0870 603 0304; www.bbc.co.uk/experience. Underground: Oxford Circus or Regent's Park. Open: Mon 1100–1800, Tue–Sun 1000–1800. Last tour at 1630. ££.

The **British Broadcasting Corporation** has a cherished place in British life, satirised as 'Auntie Beeb' for its 'mission to explain' and its tradition of putting education before entertainment. Broadcasting House, where it all started, is now the home of BBC Radio and the displays focus largely on radio at the expense of television. On the one-hour guided tour, you listen to classic radio clips (such as George V's first Christmas broadcast in 1932) and get to take part in a short radio play. Most of the fun, especially for children, comes at the end when you are left alone in an interactive area where you can try your hand at recording a sports commentary and presenting the weather forecast on TV.

Bond Street

Underground: Bond Street, Green Park or Piccadilly Circus.

Bond Street, in the heart of Mayfair, is London's most exclusive shopping street. More than anywhere else in London, this is where you can spot supermodels stepping out of chauffeured limousines and play guess-the-celebrity by following the personalised number plates.

Old Bond Street, traditionally home to art and antique dealers, is gradually being taken over by the big fashion houses, such as **Gucci**, **Prada** and **Versace**. It is hard not to be intimidated by their sleek, minimalist boutiques, full of light and space and ultra-hip doormen in black T-shirts. These days, the design makes as much of a statement as the clothes. **Dolce & Gabbana**'s new London flagship store is all red velvet curtains and black volcanic stone, while **DKNY** has a wine and juice bar and banks of video screens. For relief from all this fashion, head for the **Royal Arcade**, a Victorian iron-and-glass covered arcade with several antique shops and the chocolatiers **Charbonnel et Walker**. Also in Old Bond Street is **Tiffany & Co** (*No 25*), a branch of the famous New York jewellers.

New Bond Street is the home of London's top jewellers, including **Cartier** (*No 175*), **Chanel** (*No 173*) and **Mikimoto** (*No 179*). **Tessiers** (*No 26*) is an antique jewellers and goldsmiths, while **Asprey & Garrard** (*No 168*), the Queen's jewellers, is the shop from where Prince Charles bought Diana's engagement ring. Also in New Bond Street, look out for **Sotheby's** (*No 35*), the famous auction house and **Smythson of Bond St** (*No 40*), the most up-market stationers in London with a warrant of appointment to the Queen.

Burlington Arcade

Underground: Green Park or Piccadilly Circus.

This Regency shopping arcade, opened in 1819, is still patrolled by top-hatted 'beadles', retired members of the 10th Hussars regiment who are 'authorised to request any person to leave' for breaking the bye-laws which prohibit 'whistling, singing or hurrying'. The handsome arcade is lined with shops selling pewter, jewellery and fine English clothes, as well as others specialising in antique quills, old maps and Russian Fabergé eggs. A few of the shops are so exclusive that you need to ring on the doorbell in order to be let in. Beyond Burlington Arcade, continue into Cork Street, home to several contemporary art galleries. Savile Row, parallel to Cork Street, is a byword for gentlemen's tailoring; the shops include **Gieves & Hawkes**, bespoke tailors to the rich and famous, and **Ede & Ravenscroft**, robemakers for the Royal Family.

London Zoo

This, the first zoological society in the world, was established in 1826 by Sir Humphrey Davy, inventor of the miner's safety lamp, and Sir Stamford Raffles, the legendary founder of Singapore. Originally set up for scientific research, the zoo did not open its doors to the public until 1847, when it immediately became a popular day out.

More than 600 species of animals and birds are now on display, including 100 threatened with extinction in the wild. The big cats (Asian lions, Sumatran tigers and leopards) remain a popular draw, as do the elephants, rhinos and giraffes. Children enjoy the reptile house, the aquarium and **Moonlight World**, where nocturnal creatures are kept, as well as the children's zoo, featuring farm and domesticated animals. Among the other attractions are the Mappin Terrace, billed as 'London's only mountain' and home to sloth bears; the Penguin Pool, designed by Berthold Lubetkin in 1934; and a walk-through aviary created by **Lord Snowdon**.

Inevitably, in response to changing public attitudes, the emphasis has shifted from entertainment towards education and conservation. Gone are the days when Jumbo could be sold to the American showman **P T Barnum** for use in circus shows. The latest attraction is the **Web of Life exhibition**, a glass pavilion that is part-museum, part-live animal display, focussing on the role of biodiversity in preserving the world's ecosystems.

> *"Every passing soundbite was as captivating as the opening line from a Chekhov short story."*
>
> **Nigel Tisdall in Regent's Park, *A Walk Through London's Parks, Daily Telegraph*, 1998**

Getting there: Regent's Park. Tel: (020) 7722 3333; www.weboflife.co.uk. Underground: Camden Town, waterbus services from Camden Lock and Little Venice in summer. Open: Mar–Sept 1000–1730 daily, Oct–Feb 1000–1600 daily; closed 25 Dec and 1 Jan. £££.

Regent's Park

Underground: Baker Street, Great Portland Street or Regent's Park.
Open from dawn to dusk.

Once part of Middlesex Forest, then a royal hunting ground for **Henry VIII**, Regent's Park was laid out between 1817 and 1829 by **John Nash**, friend of the Prince Regent (later **George IV**), and is considered London's supreme example of town planning. There are rose gardens, meadows, avenues of trees, a boating lake, canalside walks and a Broad Walk from which to enjoy sweeping views of Nash's handsome Regency terraces, with the tall 1960s **Telecom Tower** looming incongruously overhead.

The path strikes the perfect balance between formal attractions and open space. Among the attractions are London Zoo, an open-air theatre where Shakespeare plays are performed in summer and a **bandstand** where concerts are given (it was here that a terrorist bomb killed seven military bandsmen in 1982). There are also several good cafés and children's playgrounds dotted around the park. Above all, though, Regent's Park is a place to stroll on a summer evening or crisp winter day, listening to the distant sounds of the zoo animals and stumbling across gems such as the white marble fountain, erected by the Metropolitan Drinking Fountain and Cattle Trough Association in 1869, a gift from Sir Cowasjee Jahangir, 'a wealthy Parsee gentleman of Bombay'.

The best of the Regency terraces are found on the east side of the park boundary, especially Chester and Cumberland Terraces, with their Corinthian pillars and white stuccoed façades. On the far side of the park, look out for the **London Central Mosque**, which opened in 1978. Visitors are welcome to go inside, but remember to dress appropriately and to take your shoes off at the door.

Madame Tussaud's

Marylebone Road. Advance bookings: (020) 7935 6861. Underground: Baker Street. Open: June–Aug, 0900–1730 daily; rest of the year Mon–Fri 1000–1730, Sat–Sun 0920–1730. Planetarium open: Mon–Fri 1220–1700, Sat–Sun and school holidays 1020–1700. £££. The queues for Madame Tussaud's and the Planetarium can be extremely long and it is well worth booking tickets in advance by credit card (for which there is no extra fee).

London's most popular paid-for attraction is crowded, commercialised and completely over the top, but also utterly absorbing. Although it has spawned imitators all over the world, a visit to Madame Tussaud's remains a genuine London experience.

It was founded by **Marie Grosholtz** (1761–1850), a modeller and tutor to the French Royal Family, who escaped execution during the French Revolution by making death masks of guillotine victims – some of whom, such as Louis XVI and Marie Antoinette, were personal friends. Eventually she escaped to England, where she exhibited her waxworks in the Lyceum Theatre in London before touring the country and establishing a museum in Baker Street, close to the present site.

A few of Madame Tussaud's original models are still on display, but for most visitors the fascination lies in coming face to face with more modern characters from the worlds of show business, films and sport. You enter through the Garden Party, where **Richard Branson** chats to **Paul Gascoigne**, **Dudley Moore** plays the piano and the cocktails are served by **Andrew Sachs**, the waiter from the popular TV comedy ***Fawlty Towers***. Visitors queue to have their photo taken with **Sean Connery**, **Ian Botham** or **Naomi Campbell**. Some of the figures are so lifelike that it is hard to know which are the models and which the tourists.

Next comes 200 Years, where discarded heads and body parts are a cruel sign of who has fallen out of favour – failed politicians, forgotten film stars and singers who have enjoyed their fifteen minutes of fame. The Hollywood Legends gallery features **Humphrey Bogart**, **Marlon Brando**, **John Wayne** and **Marilyn Monroe**, but this is merely the warm-up act for the Great Hall. Here, kings and queens of Britain from **William the Conqueror** onwards rub shoulders with US presidents, world leaders, **Shakespeare**, **Dickens** and Madame Tussaud's own model of **Voltaire** – as well as her final work, a self-portrait completed in 1842 at the age of 81.

> "*At Madame Tussaud's I had a rather unpleasant discovery; my incapacity to read human faces, or the deceptions within the faces themselves. Thus, I was at once charmed by a gentleman in a chair with a goatee. The catalogue revealed him as Thomas Neill Cream, hanged in 1892. 'Poisoned Matilda Glover with strychnine'.*"
>
> **Karel Capek (1890–1938)**

For many people, the highlight is the **Chamber of Horrors**, featuring mass murderers and grisly methods of execution – including the guillotine with which Madame Tussaud was so familiar. Those with young children should skip this exhibition and move straight on to the **Spirit of London**, an entertaining 'time ride' through London's history, complete with animatronic figures and special effects.

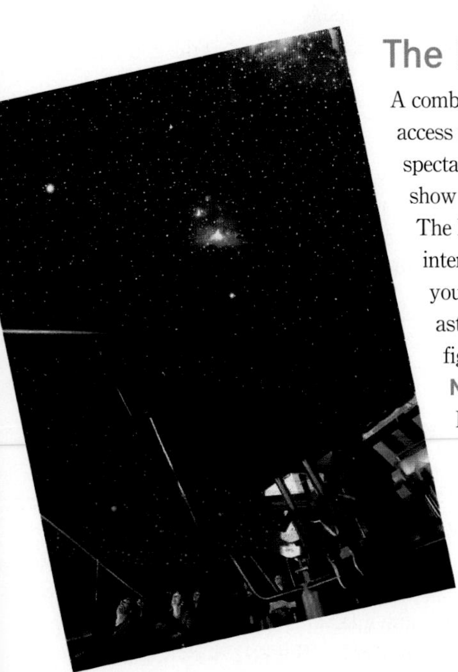

The Planetarium

A combined admission ticket gives access to the **Planetarium**, a spectacular virtual reality space show using the latest technology. The Planetarium also contains the interactive Space Zone, where you can discover the secrets of astronomy surrounded by wax figures of **Einstein**, **Galileo**, **Neil Armstrong** and the British mathematician **Stephen Hawking**.

Oxford Street

Underground: Bond Street, Marble Arch, Oxford Circus or Tottenham Court Road.

To outsiders, Oxford Street represents the bright lights of London, the most famous shopping street in the world; whereas Londoners know that, in truth, it is not what it used to be. At times, when shoppers queue for the January sales or the street is festooned with Christmas lights, it has some of its old appeal, but most of the time Oxford Street is a noisy, crowded agglomeration of tourists, pickpockets, con men and overrated shops.

Although it was the start of the road to Oxford in Roman times, the street actually takes its name from the **Earl of Oxford**, who bought the land to the north of the street in 1713. Before that, it was known as Tyburn Way because it led to the gallows at **Tyburn**, on the site of today's Marble Arch. The street was gradually developed for commerce during the 18th and 19th centuries; its status as London's chief shopping street was confirmed by the decision of American entrepreneur Gordon Selfridge to build his department store there in 1908.

Selfridges (*No 400*) is still one of London's leading department stores, with three floors of fashions and an excellent food hall. With its huge Ionic columns and art-deco clock, the shop is an instantly recognisable Oxford Street landmark. Near here is the flagship branch of **Marks &**

Spencer (*No 458*), known for its reliable, own-brand clothes. Many of their new lines come on sale here before moving to other branches. Other good department stores are dependable **John Lewis** (*Nos 278–306*), whose motto is 'never knowingly undersold', and **Debenhams** (*Nos 334–48*), which once had a reputation for mediocrity but has managed to move up-market while retaining its competitive prices.

Apart from the department stores, there are few shops worth a special trip. **Top Shop** (*No 214*) at Oxford Circus, a mecca for London's teenagers, claims to be the biggest fashion store in the world, while nearby **Niketown** is more of a lifestyle statement than a shoe shop. Continuing east, there are two good music megastores, **HMV** (*No 150*) and **Virgin** (*Nos 14–16*), with a huge range of CDs, videos and games, plus the American-style book megastore **Borders** (*Nos 203–7*), but for the most part this is a dreary stretch of electronics shops, souvenir emporia and last year's fashions.

To escape the relentless pressure, seek out **Gees Court** and **St Christopher's Place**, a pair of narrow pedestrian alleys entered through a tiny archway on the north side of the street between James Street and Stratford Place. With their pavement cafés and small, quirky shops selling everything from model soldiers to children's shoes, this feels more like a little bit of Covent Garden.

The Wallace Collection

Not far from here, in the 18th-century Hertford House, the **Wallace Collection** (*Manchester Square; tel: (020) 7935 0687; open: Mon–Sat 1000–1700, Sun 1400–1700; £*) is one of London's best-kept secrets. The private collection of Sir Richard Wallace, illegitimate son of the 4th Marquess of Hertford, this contains paintings by **Rubens**, **Rembrandt** and **Velázquez**, portraits by **Gainsborough** and **Reynolds**, 18th-century French furniture, **Sèvres** porcelain and a fine collection of European armour. Following a £10 million refit, the collection is due to be reopened as a national museum in June 2000, with four new galleries and a glass roof over the courtyard.

Piccadilly

Piccadilly takes its name from a family mansion built here in 1612 by Robert Baker, a Somerset tailor who made his fortune selling stiff collars known as 'pickadills'. These days Piccadilly, running from Hyde Park to Shaftesbury Avenue, combines elements of aristocratic Mayfair, old-fashioned St James's and gaudy Soho.

Start at Green Park tube station, and look across to the **Ritz Hotel**, which opened in 1906 and has long been a favourite haunt of the rich and fashionable. It is still the best place in London to take a traditional afternoon tea, with scones, pastries and cucumber sandwiches. Further east is **Fortnum & Mason**, the grocery store founded in 1707 by William Fortnum, footman to the royal household, and Hugh Mason, a shopkeeper of St James's. The ground floor, with its chandeliers and gilded ceilings, is a food-lover's fantasy, selling smoked salmon and caviar, cheeses and fine wines. Downstairs, in the basement, you can order a Fortnum's hamper, just the thing for a summer picnic or a day at the races.

Across the street, Burlington House is an 18th-century Palladian mansion, remodelled in the 19th century in Italian Renaissance style. This is the home of the **Royal Academy** (*tel: (020) 7300 8000; open: 1000–1800 daily, 1000–2030 Fri; £££*), the most prestigious fine arts society in Britain.

Piccadilly Circus

Piccadilly ends at Piccadilly Circus, once a handsome junction designed by John Nash, now a poor imitation of New York's Times Square, with its neon lights, theme restaurants and virtual reality tourist attractions. The statue of Eros, the god of love, erected in 1892 on top of a drinking fountain, is a popular meeting-place.

A statue of the first president, Sir Joshua Reynolds, stands in the courtyard; early students included **John Constable** and **J M W Turner**. The Royal Academy is known for the quality of its art exhibitions, which attract loans from major museum collections all over the world. Also popular is the annual **Summer Exhibition**, the world's largest 'open' exhibition for living artists. Tickets for the more popular exhibitions are always at a premium, though you can book in advance in the Front Hall or through Ticketmaster (*tel: (020) 7413 1717*). You can also take a tour of the Fine Rooms, home to the permanent collection, which includes paintings by former academicians such as **Reynolds** and **Thomas Gainsborough** (*Tue–Fri 1300*). One item which is always on display is **Michelangelo**'s sculpture *Madonna and Child*, exhibited on the top floor outside Norman Foster's Sackler Wing.

Back on the south side, **St James's Church**, designed by Sir Christopher Wren in 1676, contains intricate woodcarving by Grinling Gibbons. The church has become a popular meeting-place, with lunchtime concerts, a garden café and a craft market (*Wed–Sat*). Nearby, **Hatchards** (*No 187*) is the royal booksellers, established in 1797. It has recently been dwarfed by **Waterstones** (*Nos 203–6; open: 0800–2300 daily; Sun 1200–1800*), the largest bookshop in Europe, which has opened in the former Simpson's department store. With a juice bar, an Internet station and a café where you can browse through magazines, plus entire floors devoted to fiction and children's books, you could spend all day in here. Regular author events and book signings are held on the top floor.

Getting there: Underground: Green Park, Hyde Park Corner or Piccadilly Circus.

Regent Street

Named after the Prince Regent, later ***George IV****, Regent Street was designed by the architect* ***John Nash*** *as a grand boulevard linking the aristocratic mansions of St James's with his own masterpiece at Regent's Park.*

As one of London's best-known shopping streets, Regent Street is now aimed firmly at the middle market, bridging the gap between the tackiness of neighbouring Oxford Street and the fashion fascism of Bond Street. There are pockets of serious style here, but most of the shops are solid and dependable rather than overly exciting. Among the highlights are several smart menswear shops and a row of superstores for children.

It is best to start at the Oxford Circus end and walk down the Soho side of the street, where most of the best shops are situated. **Laura Ashley** (*Nos 256–8*) was a 1960s fashion icon, known for her frilly, floral dresses, but the designs these days tend to be rather more sober. Next comes **Dickins & Jones** (*Nos 224–44*), a stylish department store with a very feminine feel, with perfume and cosmetics on the ground floor, designer clothing and lingerie, personal shoppers and a beauty parlour. There is also a grooming and tailoring service for men. Across the street, **Godiva** (*No 247*) is an up-market Belgian chocolatier with a tempting range of pralines, truffles and chocolate gifts.

Passing **Liberty's** (*Nos 210–20; see page 83*), you come to **Hamleys** (*Nos 188–96*), which claims to be the largest toyshop in the world. It has five floors of everything from model railways to computer games and a Sega amusement arcade in the basement. Hamleys has spawned a miniature children's shopping district, with **Warner Brothers Studio Store** (*Nos 178–82*) joined by the **Disney Store** (*Nos 140–4*). **Gymboree** (*No 198*) sells eye-catching clothes for designer kids, while **The English Teddy Bear Co** (*No 153*) is heaven for soft toys.

Levi's (*No 174*) sells jeans, of course, but also features a contemporary art gallery and a sound system with regular club nights and live bands. Such modernity would be unthinkable at **Mappin & Webb** (*No 170*), the Queen's silversmiths, a good place to buy silver cufflinks and hairbrushes. The lower end of the street, as you approach The Quadrant, has several shops for the man about town who cannot quite afford the prices of nearby Savile Row. **Burberry** (*No 165*), known for its very English trenchcoats and check-patterned scarves, has recently gone all trendy and is now a designer label. **Austin Reed** (*Nos 103–13*) sells classic, affordable business suits, while **Aquascutum** (*No 100*) features traditional rainwear and outdoor clothes for shooting and fishing weekends in the country. If you happen to be invited to a society wedding, **Moss Bros** (*No 88*) is the place to hire a morning suit.

The **Café Royal** (*No 68*) is a good place to meet for a glass of champagne before going to a West End show. First opened in 1865, this was once one of the most fashionable restaurants in London, the *beau monde* haunt of writers and artists such as **Oscar Wilde** and his lover Lord Alfred Douglas.

Getting there: Underground: Oxford Circus or Piccadilly Circus.

“I love London society! I think it has immensely improved. It is entirely composed now of beautiful idiots and brilliant lunatics. Just what society should be.”

Oscar Wilde, *An Ideal Husband*, 1895

Shopping

*For descriptions of the main shopping streets, see the entries for Bond Street (*see pages 58–9*), Oxford Street (*see pages 64–5*), Piccadilly (*see pages 66–7*) and Regent Street (*see pages 68–9*). It is worth seeking out some of the smaller streets within this rectangle, such as* **Cork Street** *with its art galleries and* **Savile Row** *with its tailors.*

Restaurants

L'Autre

5B Shepherd Street. Tel: (020) 7499 4680. £. This cosy Polish-Mexican bistro is typical of the eateries to be found in **Shepherd Market**, a bohemian enclave which was the original 'May Fair'. The menu features Polish classics such as *borscht, blinis* and smoked salmon, as well as spicy Mexican cuisine.

Criterion

224 Piccadilly. Tel: (020) 7930 0488. ££. This splendid mock-Byzantine ballroom, with its mosaic ceilings and wooden floors, has been transformed by chef **Marco Pierre White** into an elegant brasserie serving modern French and British cuisine at affordable prices.

Le Gavroche

43 Upper Brook Street. Tel: (020) 7408 0881. £££. **Michel Roux** has taken over from father Albert at London's top French restaurant. You could easily spend a fortune here, but the set lunch with wine is a relative bargain, and the cheeseboard and wine list (both all-French) are probably the best in London.

Hard Rock Café

150 Old Park Lane. Tel: (020) 7629 0382. ££. The original theme restaurant still has its legendary queues, loud music, rock memorabilia and a menu that is heavy on the burgers, fries and ice cream. No bookings.

Langan's Brasserie

Stratton Street. Tel: (020) 7491 8822. £££. The founder Peter Langan was famous for his love of champagne and cigars, and the Bond Street set still gather here for up-market versions of English classics such as potted shrimps, bangers and mash and apple crumble.

Momo

25 Heddon Street. Tel: (020) 7434 4040. ££. With cushions, candlelight and hypnotic music, this trendy **Moroccan** restaurant has all the feel of Marrakech. The North African menu features several varieties of *couscous* and *tajine*, while the Mô café next door is a cross between a tearoom and an Arabic bazaar.

Oak Room

Meridien Hotel, 21 Piccadilly. Tel: (020) 7437 0202. £££. This is the restaurant where **Marco Pierre White**, the *enfant terrible* of Cool Britannia London, gained his third Michelin star. He has now retired from the kitchen but retains overall control and the restaurant still turns out classic French haute cuisine. White's talent is also on display at **Mirabelle** (*56 Curzon Street; tel: (020) 7499 4636; ££*), where dishes such as omelette Arnold Bennett and grilled lemon sole come at marginally more affordable prices.

Rasa

6 Dering Street. Tel: (020) 7629 1346. ££. This smart **Indian** restaurant off Oxford Street serves the vegetarian home cooking of Kerala. The starter of mixed snacks and chutneys sets the tone, followed by several unusual curries such as beetroot and spinach or mango with green bananas.

St Marylebone Café

17 Marylebone Road. Tel: (020) 7935 6374. £. For a good-value lunch close to Madame Tussaud's, you won't do better than this vegetarian café in the crypt of St Marylebone Church. Choices include soup, salad, quiche and a daily hot dish.

Veeraswamy

101 Regent Street. Tel: (020) 7734 1401. ££. London's oldest Indian restaurant has shaken off its fusty Raj image and been transformed into an elegant, modern hangout serving everything from Bombay street food to authentic regional Indian cuisine.

Afternoon tea

There can be few more English traditions than afternoon tea in one of Mayfair's top hotels. The menus feature dainty sandwiches, scones with cream and a selection of cakes, and although prices are steep, you will not need to eat again all day. Entertainment is provided by a pianist or string quartet. The classic place to take tea is at the ***Ritz*** *(* 150 Piccadilly; tel: (020) 7493 8181 *), though you may need to book at least a month in advance. Others are* ***Brown's*** *(* 33 Albemarle Street; tel: (020) 7518 4108 *),* ***Claridge's*** *(* Brook Street; tel: (020) 7629 8860 *) and the* ***Dorchester*** *(* 54 Park Lane; tel: (020) 7629 8888 *). Most hotels impose a dress code, so remember to ask when you book.*

PROFILE

Village London

It has often been said that London is really just a collection of villages. The megalopolis of today was never planned; instead it has grown organically, with areas that were once surrounded by farmland gradually sucked into the urban sprawl. A character in a **Tobias Smollett** *novel remarked in 1771, after seven years out of London, that 'what I left open fields, producing hay and corn, I now find covered with streets and squares ... Pimlico and Knightsbridge are almost joined to Chelsea and Kensington'. Much the same could be said of Kingston or Greenwich today.*

Yet despite the sprawl, the essential identity of the different villages remains. To the north, **Camden**, **Islington** and **Hampstead** are arty, fashionable places, beloved of literary types and left-leaning politicians (the Prime Minister, Tony Blair, had a house in Islington). South of the river, **Dulwich** and **Camberwell** are sedate, middle-class villages, with steep hills, Georgian houses, commons and village greens. Like **Richmond** and **Wimbledon** to the west, they are semi-detached from London, looking outwards to the rural commuter belt of golf courses and mock-Tudor mansions as much as inwards to the city. Yet even in the heart of London you find authentic village communities, in unlikely places such as **Soho**, or

Mayfair's **Shepherd Market**, a maze of alleys, lanes and mews cottages with a raffish, bohemian atmosphere where high-class prostitutes mingle with diplomats, dukes and spies.

The growth of London as a multi-ethnic city has led to pockets of foreign culture springing up across the city. **Brixton**, with its large Afro-Caribbean community, is home to one of London's liveliest street markets, a good place to buy African fabrics, reggae music, plantains or dried fish, while newly fashionable **Notting Hill** is renowned for its summer carnival. **Brick Lane**, in the East End, has become known as 'Banglatown' because of its large Bengali population, who support numerous mosques, sari shops and curry houses. The Jewish community has traditionally gathered in **Whitechapel** and **Golders Green**, the Portuguese in **Vauxhall**, while **Southall** in west London is home to a large Indian population. In 1995 the largest Hindu temple outside India, built in India from Carrara marble and shipped back to London, opened in the nearby suburb of **Neasden**.

> *"The secret of enjoying this place is to break the city down and see it as a collection of villages, each with a distinct character."*
>
> **Fergal Keane, *The Independent*, 1999**

Soho and Bloomsbury

Soho has London's theatreland, Chinatown, its red-light district, its gay quarter and scores of specialist bookshops, plus colourful markets and the hub of Britain's film and TV industry. Sober Bloomsbury has the scholarly institutions of the British Library and the British Museum. So, somewhere to study by day and play by night.

Soho and Bloomsbury

Getting there: Soho is served by Oxford Circus, Tottenham Court Road, Piccadilly Circus and Leicester Square ***tubes****, the latter being the most central. Most* ***buses*** *pass through the area: take any bus that says Piccadilly or Oxford Circus on its indicator board. For the British Museum, go to Holborn, Russell Square or Tottenham Court Road tube and walk; buses 7, 10, 55 and 98 pass close by the museum doors. The British Library is equidistant between Euston Square, Euston and King's Cross tube stations and on the route of buses 10, 30 and 73. For Camden Lock, take the tube to Camden Town and walk, or take buses 24, 27 or 168.*

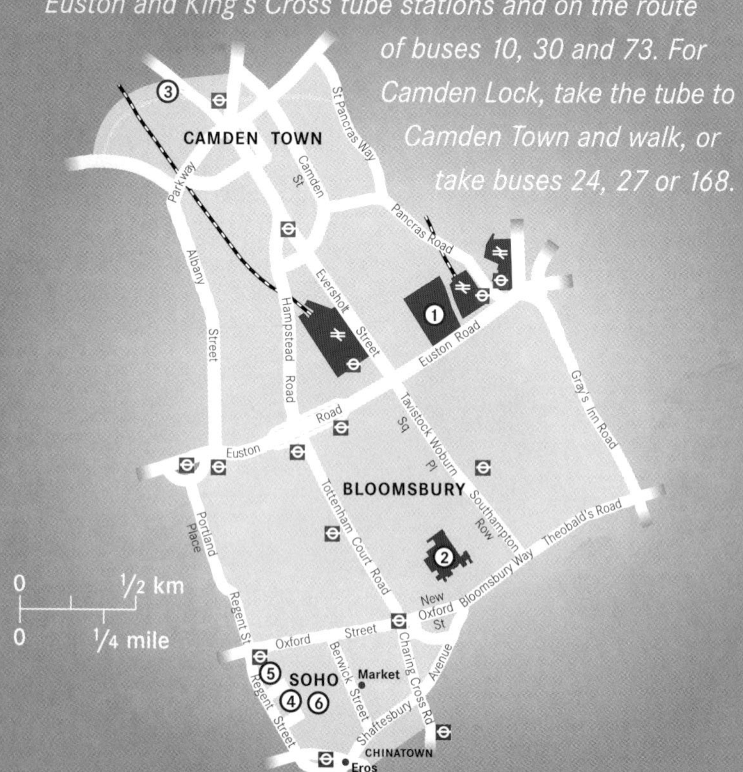

① *British Library*

For bookish visitors this is a treat: the hallowed home of some of the world's oldest and most influential books and manuscripts, from early illuminated bibles and **Shakespeare** first editions to **Leonardo da Vinci**'s notebooks and **the Beatles** early lyrics. Page 79

② *British Museum*

Antiquities from around the world fill the galleries of this venerable museum – the first of its kind in the world and one of the largest. From the painted **mummies** of ancient Egypt to complete **Grecian temples**, the sheer scale of the museum is awesome – and it continues to grow, with the long-awaited opening of the central Great Court due very soon. Pages 80–1

③ *Camden Lock Market*

Call it hippy, call it New Age, this is where idealistic youth meets consumer power in a easy-going atmospheric market selling homemade crafts, food, clothes and jewellery. Fun without too much expense. Page 82

④ *Carnaby Street*

Synonymous with the Swinging Sixties, Carnaby Street has continued to evolve with the times and to reflect whatever trend is hip and cool. Some dismiss it as tacky, but it's very much a part of the Soho scene. Pages 82–3

⑤ *Liberty*

Yes, it's a store but you could forgive anyone who thought it was a museum or a souk in some fantastic fairy-tale. Enjoy the mock-Tudor building and admire handicrafts from Africa, Asia and the Arab world. Page 83

⑥ *Soho*

Soho is for people watching, nightlife and lounging in cafés. It's as close as London gets to a **bohemian Left Bank**, with its pot-pourri mix of continental food shops and Chinese supermarkets; its porn shops and its pubs where ageing journalists wreck their livers; its bookshops and its tiny restaurants where Internet entrepreneurs, filmmakers and advertising executives discuss their latest schemes to get rich. Page 78

Tip

Thursday is late-night shopping night in this area, when shops stay open until 1900 or 1930.

Soho and Chinatown

Soho has few formal sights and attractions, but is a great place for wandering with no particular aim except to indulge the senses with an array of tastes, sights and sounds.

Food lovers will enjoy the wonderful selection of delicatessen shops and cafés in **Old Compton Street**, or the authentic French coffee and pâtisseries of **Valerie** or **Maison Bertaux** in **Greek Street**. One block north is **Berwick Street**, home of one of London's best open-air food markets. Go three blocks south, crossing Shaftesbury Avenue, and you will travel from the European continent to Hong Kong: **Gerrard Street** is the focus of London's **Chinatown**, where everything, from the smells, and the colourful fruits, vegetables and live fish on display, is all tantalisingly strange and foreign and where you can eat Chinese food as authentic as any that Canton itself can offer.

Historically, Soho has always been the home of refugees and émigrés, especially those from eastern Europe, and they have brought a taste for books as well as for good food. Individual shops come and go, but **Charing Cross Road**, on Soho's eastern edge, remains the focus for scores of specialist shops. **Foyles** (*Nos 113–19*) is the biggest of them all and the most confusingly old-fashioned: you may need help to locate a book, but the chances are that, if it's in print, they have it (and they have an excellent art gallery as well). On the opposite side of the road, heading south, **Zwemmers** (*Nos 72 and 80*) is one of the best shops anywhere for books on art, architecture, film and photography and other nearby shops specialise in second-hand and antiquarian books.

British Library

96 Euston Road. Tel: (020) 7412 7332; www.bl.uk. Open: Mon and Wed–Fri 0930–1800; Tue 0930–2000; Sat 0930–1700; Sun 1100–1700; closed 24–28 Dec and 1 Jan. £.

Once located in the famous Round Reading Room at the British Museum, the British Library moved out to these purpose-built premises in 1998. Scholars come here to consult the BL's **unique reference collection** (books cannot be loaned), covering every book or journal published in the UK. Everyone is welcome to visit the library and explore the building, its sculpture-filled piazza (with music and free events in summer) and its three exhibition galleries.

The stars of the collection are displayed in the **John Ritblat Gallery**. Some 200 books and manuscripts are on permanent display and there is a special kind of thrill to be had from reading the handwriting of **Dickens**, **Lewis Carroll** or **Jane Austen**, complete with second thoughts, crossings-out and amendments. The collection ranges in date from **Paul McCartney**'s lyrics for *Yesterday*, to the gorgeously illuminated **Lindisfarne Gospels** (*c* AD 698) and includes manuscripts or early editions of *Beowulf* and the *Canterbury Tales*, *The Jungle Book* and **Handel**'s *Messiah*, **Captain Scott's diary** and a letter from **Mahatma Gandhi**.

The **Pearson Gallery** and the adjacent workshop are concerned with the technology of printing and the way it has changed over the centuries. Interactive displays allow you to use desk-top design programmes to create your own book and there are regular hands-on demonstrations of printing and bookbinding aimed at children as well as adults. The **Philatelic Exhibition** has changing displays: expect to see rare early stamps, but also fine examples of modern commemorative stamp design.

British Museum

Great Russell Street. Tel: (020) 7636 1555; www.british-museum.ac.uk. Open: Mon–Sat 1000–1700; Sun 1200–1800; closed 24–26 and 31 Dec, 1 Jan and Easter Sunday. £.

Famously, the British Museum has been embroiled for decades in controversy over the 5th-century BC sculptures from the Parthenon in Athens. Lord Elgin 'rescued' them from the ruined Temple of Athena in the 19th century and Greece now wants them back.

Heretical it may be to say this, but the **Elgin Marbles** are far from being the most visually arresting of the treasures on display in the museum. The average visitor would probably be happy to hand them back, but would there be anything left in the BM if this policy were pursued to its logical conclusion?

Perhaps the BM could hang on to the marvellous objects on display in the galleries devoted to **Medieval and Later Antiquities** (*Rooms 41–47*). But no, the people of the Hebridean island of Lewis have made it clear that they want the return of their exquisite Viking-Age **Chessmen**, carved from walrus ivory in the 12th century. Fortunately there is no modern town of Sutton Hoo, so the **Sutton Hoo Treasures**, including the gorgeous garnet-inlaid regalia of Redwald, the 7th-century King of the East Angles, may not have to be relinquished.

On the other hand, many a provincial museum curator would be glad to have back the objects that make up the **Prehistoric and Romano-British** galleries (*Rooms 37 and 49–50*). For decades, the choicest archaeological finds have been requisitioned by the BM so that the galleries provide an overview of the very richest and best material found in these islands, from Bronze-Age mirrors and golden torques to the Late Roman mosaic floor from Lullingstone depicting Christ in Majesty. The star of the show, though, is **Pete Marsh**, aptly named by archaeologists who found his well-preserved 2,000-year-old body in a waterlogged bog in Cheshire.

Egypt and Asia

Many of the Egyptian treasures in the museum were looted – not by museum staff, you must understand, but by French soldiers, rampaging across Europe and North Africa during the French Revolution and Napoleonic eras. They 'liberated' numerous antiquities, which were then seized by the victorious British. That is how the celebrated **Rosetta Stone** came to be here (*Room 25*), carved with the same text in hieroglyphics and ancient Greek, thus supplying the means to understanding ancient Egyptian pictograms. It stands amongst a collection of objects of astonishing richness that build up a picture of an apparently idyllic life in the land of the Pharaohs.

By contrast, life in **Nineveh** seems to have been one long battle, with dire consequences for the losers. The intricately carved Assyrian friezes in the **Western Asiatic** department are covered in vignettes of warfare, sieges, victory processions and nasty scenes of torture and death that will appeal to little boys hooked on gory computer games.

Imagine all this gone. What would be left, of course, is the building itself which is being revealed in all its glory as work progresses on the restoration of the **Great Court** and the **Round Reading Room** at the heart of the museum. New shops and restaurants, galleries and lecture theatres, multimedia interpretation centres and educational resources are planned for what will surely become one of the most exciting public spaces in London.

Camden Lock Market

What began as an *ad-hoc* market started by a group of idealistic hippies in the 1970s has developed into one of London's top tourist attractions and has spread well beyond its original location. The spirit of the original market is still represented by the wholefood stalls and handmade crafts of The Lock, a cobbled courtyard alongside the **Grand Union Canal** four blocks north of Camden Town tube station. The open-air market only opens at the weekend (*Sat and Sun 1000–1800*) but there are permanent stalls in the surrounding warehouse and stable buildings (*open: Tue–Sun 1000–1800*) and there is a general street market in Buck Street, just to the south (*open: Thur–Sun 0800–1800*), where the bargains on offer range from antique clothing and second-hand books to bric-à-brac, posters and furniture.

Carnaby Street

Running parallel with busy Regent Street, Carnaby Street is a pedestrian enclave which draws young visitors to London, partly because of its cheap clothes shops and partly for the nostalgia. This was the heart of London in the **Swinging**

Sixties, the place where everyone came to buy joss sticks and paisley shirts, Afghan coats and bellbottom trousers. Since the same shops sold equipment for smoking marijuana and experimental magazines then judged to be obscene, they were regularly raided by the police. Maybe Carnaby Street has lost its youthful cutting edge, but it's still a place where people like to hang out in warm weather, with a choice of pavement cafés, several American-style coffee shops and the Shakespeare's Head, the pub at the Oxford Street end of the street with a bust of Shakespeare set in a niche above the door.

Liberty

Great Marlborough Street. Tel: (020) 7734 1234; www.liberty-of-london.com. Open: Mon–Wed 1000–1830; Thur to 2000; Fri and Sat to 1900; closed Sun.

Spend a while admiring Liberty's exterior before plunging into the exotic bazaar-like interior. The attention-grabbing window displays provide a quick snapshot of what's cool and trendy in fashion and accessories, whilst the building above is a wonderful example of backwards-looking nostalgia. Dating from 1924, the Tudor-style store was built from ships' timbers salvaged from HMS *Impregnable* and HMS *Hindustan*. Like the gilded caravel that serves as a weather-vane high above the Great Marlborough Street entrance, and the frieze of Britannia receiving gifts from around the world over the Regent Street entrance, the symbolism here is redolent of the great age of discovery, when ships would return laden with exotic goods from distant lands.

True to the founder's vision, Liberty still manages to excite and delight shoppers with its own inimitable brand of stylish exoticism. Take the lift to the top floor and look over the balcony of the great stairwell to see a cascade of **colourful rugs and fabrics**. From here you can descend floor by floor discovering the delights of Arts-and-Crafts antiques (silver and pewter, furniture and sculpture), oriental rugs, an excellent art gallery and café, designer clothes, jewellery, crafts and fashion accessories and a basement packed with gift ideas and stylish goods for the bath, kitchen and home.

Shopping

As well as Carnaby Street and Liberty (*see pages 82–3*), the other main shopping focus in this area is **Tottenham Court Road**, which has electronics shops competing to sell you discounted laptops, games consoles and stereo systems at the southern end and top-quality interior furnishing stores from the midpoint northwards. Two must-see stores in the same building (*196 Tottenham Court Road*) are **Heals** (*tel: (020) 7636 1666; closed Sun*), selling a representative cross-section of modern British and European design, but with a definite bias towards Arts-and-Crafts style, and **Habitat** (*tel: (020) 7631 3880; open daily*) for affordable mass-manufactured design. On the opposite side of the road is **Purves & Purves**, which always has fresh and inspiring furnishing ideas (*80–3 Tottenham Court Road; tel: (020) 7580 8223; closed Sun*).

Nightlife

With London's theatreland on the doorstep, the choice of live drama is unlimited, though getting **tickets** at short notice is not easy. The best bet is to try the ticket agencies along Shaftesbury Road, or phone an agency such as **First Call** (*tel: (020) 7420 0000*). Alternatively, try the **Half-Price Ticket Booth** on the south side of Leicester Square where unsold tickets for that day's performances are available to cash payers at bargain prices (*open: Mon–Sat 1200–1830, Sun 1200–1500; two tickets per person; expect to queue*).

Clubs in Soho come and go, but **Ronnie Scott's** (*47 Frith Street; tel: (020) 7439 0747; open: Mon–Sat 2030–0300; ££*) seems to go from strength to strength. Founded in 1959, it represents the unchanging soul of Soho, drawing some of the world's most accomplished **jazz** performers.

Soho is also Gay London's capital. **Freedom** (*60–6 Wardour Street; tel: (020) 7734 0071*) is one of several gay bars with a mixed, relaxed and welcoming atmosphere, whereas **Candy Bar** is strictly for the girls, with a bar and downstairs disco (*4 Carlisle Street; tel: (020) 7494 4041*).

Eating and drinking

Soho is the perfect place to come and eat. There is so much choice that you don't have to set out with a destination in mind: just browse the menus posted outside and then choose a restaurant that suits your pocket and tastes.

The Old Compton Street area has every type of restaurant, from the inspired Mediterranean-influenced cooking of **Alastair Little** (*49 Frith Street; tel: (020) 7734 5183; £££*) to the cheap and wholesome nosh at **Stockpot**, where a full meal costs under £10 (*18 Old Compton Street; tel: (020) 7287 1066; £*).

Eminent gourmet temples such as **L'Escargot** (*48 Greek Street; tel: (020) 7437 2679; £££*), serving serious French food against a backdrop of Picasso sketches, coexist with breezy newcomers such as **Hi Sushi**, the cheerily Japanese canteen dishing up sushi and noodles, and with a good-value 'Top of the Pops' menu that lets you sample a range of different dishes (*40 Frith Street; tel: (020) 7734 9688; ££*).

Soho is fuelled by coffee and though there are the usual espresso chains to choose from, locals prefer the old-fashioned ambience of **Pâtisserie Valerie**, where excellent coffee is accompanied by sandwiches, salads and their trade-mark cakes (*44 Old Compton Street; tel: (020) 7437 3466; closes 2000 Mon–Fri, 1900 Sat and 1800 Sun; £*).

If this is too full or too busy for your liking, head for the **Maison Bertaux**, where the service can be slow and offhand but the croissant, pastries and savouries would meet the approval of any discerning Gaul (*28 Greek Street; tel: (020) 7437 6007; open till 2000 daily; £*).

Lovers of Chinese food will find every style of cuisine in the Wardour Street/Gerrard Street area, from Cantonese-style canteens selling cheap rice, veg and *charsiu* pork or roast duck for under £5, to Peking restaurants serving multi-course imperial banquets.

Chuen Cheng Ku specialises in *dim sum* (served until 1745; full meals after that) and the menu comes with helpful photographs and descriptions – great if you want to try lots of new tastes (*17 Wardour Street; tel: (020) 7437 1398; ££*). The **Jade Garden** strives to recreate pre-war Shanghai with jazz and period décor (*15 Wardour Street; tel: (020) 7437 5065; ££*) but the Chinatown restaurant that draws most plaudits from connoisseurs is **New Diamond** (*23 Lisle Street; tel: (020) 7437 2517; ££*), where seafood (steamed bass, scallops) features prominently and where the brave go for the Chinese Specials menu.

Islington

Restaurants and theatres abound in Islington, along with estate agents selling expensive flats in a part of London that is greatly in demand because it offers elegant town houses within walking distance (almost) of the City and West End.

The fortunes of Islington are symbolised by the **Quality Chop House** at 94 Farringdon Road (*tel: (020) 7837 5093; £££*), a former working-class caff that retains its original bench seats and narrow tables, but now serves caviar and roast monkfish (*see page 118*). Gentrification has seen the butchers, bakers and fishmongers of nearby **Exmouth Market** give way to Japanese noodle bars, Seattle-style coffee shops and smart Italian *ristorante*. This is where theatre-goers come for sustenance before visiting **Sadler's Wells Theatre**, on Rosebery Avenue, an exciting modern glass-and-steel building renowned for hosting world-class ballet, modern dance and opera (*tel: (020) 7863 8000; www.sadlers-wells.com*).

A short way north, on busy Pentonville Street, the **Crafts Council** occupies a converted chapel (*No 44A; tel: (020) 7278 7700, www.craftscouncil.org.uk; open: Tue–Sat 1100–1800, Sun 1400–1800, closed Mon*) and has a gallery, reference library, shop and café under one roof. Here you can sit and browse through a computer database of the best of British crafts.

Core Islington begins just north of here, at Upper Street and Islington Green. On the left, set back from the broad raised pavement, is the glass-and-steel Agricultural Hall of 1862, now the **Business Design Centre** and a major exhibition centre with a stunning interior. Beyond this point, Upper Street and its offshoots are lined with restaurants (*for a full listing, see www.discover-islington.co.uk*), from the **Afghan Kitchen**, which serves simple vegetarian food (*35 Islington Green; tel: (020) 7359 8019; £*) to **Granita** (*127 Upper Street; tel: (020) 7226 3222; ££*), serving sophisticated Mediterranean food and the former haunt of Prime Minister Tony Blair.

On the opposite side of the road, **Camden Passage** looks like the set for a film version of a Dickens novel. The elegant 18th-century houses lining the alley form the backdrop to a huge antiques market, crammed with over 300 shops and stalls, which takes place on Wed and Sat, with a book market on Thurs (but covered stalls are open daily).

If you want to find out all about life inside houses such as these, visit the excellent **Geffrye Museum**, on the eastern fringes of Islington (*Kingsland Road; tel: (020) 7739 9893; open: Tue–Sat 1000–1700, Sun 1200–1700, closed Mon; £*). One of London's most fascinating and relaxed museums, this consists of a series of rooms furnished in period style from the Tudor age to the present day, plus a laid-back coffee shop where you can browse through art and design magazines and a good series of design-related temporary exhibitions.

Covent Garden and Holborn

From Trafalgar Square to Covent Garden, this area beats to the pulse of its buskers, entertainers, open-air cafés and quirky shops.

COVENT GARDEN AND HOLBORN

BEST OF

Covent Garden and Holborn

*Getting there: the most useful **underground** stations are Charing Cross, Covent Garden and Leicester Square for Covent Garden and Chancery Lane, Holborn and Temple for Holborn. **Buses** 11 and 15 connect Trafalgar Square with the Strand and Fleet Street, linking most of the attractions in this chapter.*

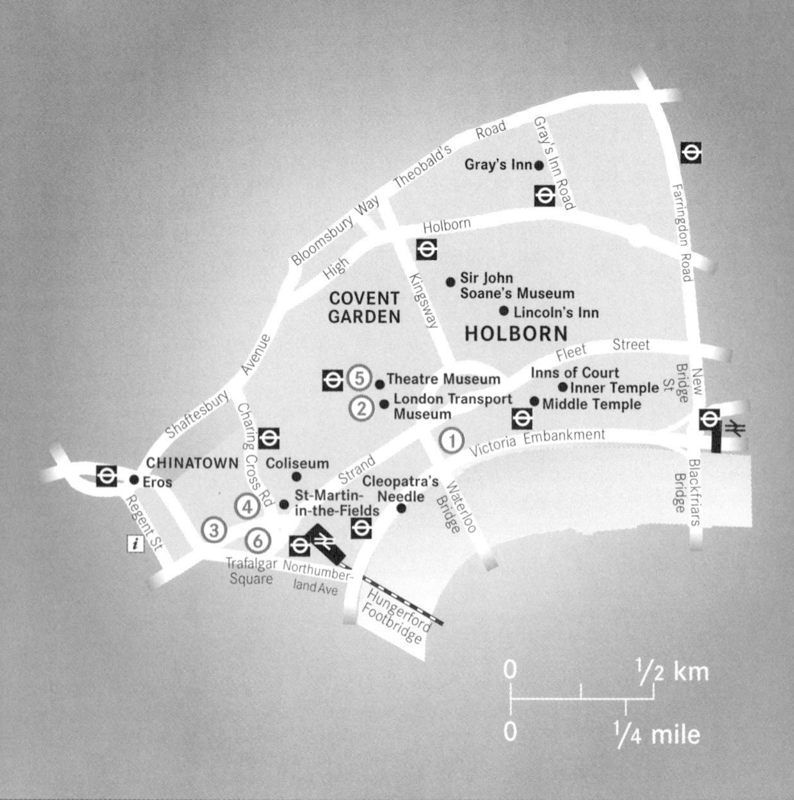

① *Courtauld Gallery*

The finest small art gallery in London is more like a private collection, with a remarkable display of Impressionist and Post-Impressionist paintings. It is located in Somerset House, a riverside palace newly restored to its 18th-century splendour. **Pages 92–3**

② *Covent Garden Piazza*

The apple carts have been replaced by jewellery stalls and the market pubs are now espresso bars, but with its buskers, gypsies and flower sellers this square still conjures up something of the atmosphere of a medieval bazaar. **Pages 94–5**

③ *National Gallery*

The national collection of West European art is quite simply the finest art gallery in the country, with works by all the major artists of the last 700 years. Admission is free, so you don't have to see it all in one go. **Pages 98–9**

④ *National Portrait Gallery*

If you're struggling to come to terms with British history, watch it come alive through the faces of kings, queens, soldiers, explorers, courtiers and courtesans down the ages. There are paintings, sculptures and photographs, but every single item is a portrait. **Page 100**

⑤ *Royal Opera House*

The magnificent Victorian opera house has been restored to its former glory and is once again staging lavish productions. The building has been opened up to the public for the first time and is becoming a popular daytime meeting-point. **Page 95**

⑥ *Trafalgar Square*

The closest thing in London to a central square, this is where celebrations, rallies and political demonstrations take place. **Nelson's Column**, with its bronze lions, is an instantly recognisable London landmark. **Pages 106–7**

Tip

The area around Covent Garden is buzzing day and night, seven days a week. Strangely, the easiest time to get a restaurant table is often between 2000–2200 in the evening, when everyone else is at the theatre or opera.

Courtauld Gallery and Somerset House

Somerset House, the Strand. Tel: (020) 7873 2526; www.courtauld.ac.uk. Underground: Covent Garden, Embankment or Temple. Open: Mon–Sat 1000–1800; Sun 1200–1800; closed 24–26 Dec and 1 Jan. £ (children free). Free admission on Mondays 1000–1400.

Somerset House was designed in 1776 by **Sir William Chambers**, architect to **George III**, as the largest ever group of purpose-built public buildings in Britain. It housed, among others, the Navy Office, Stamp Office, Salt Office and the Office of the Treasurer's Remembrancer. To many UK residents, **Somerset House** also means the headquarters of the dreaded **Inland Revenue**, the body responsible for collecting Britain's taxes.

Somerset House still houses a number of government offices, but after a £35-million restoration project, it has now been thrown open to the public. The **Great Court**, a vast central courtyard, is used for free open-air concerts and the building houses an exhibition devoted to its own history. Most exciting of all, the handsome **River Terrace** is open to the public for the first time in 100 years, part of a new pedestrian link running from the South Bank to Covent Garden. With cafés on the promenade and a new waterfront museum, this is all part of London's plan to open up the river to the city.

The **Courtauld Gallery** is located on the right of the entrance arch, in the Strand Block, originally home to the Royal Academy, Royal Society and Society of Antiquaries.

> “*London, that great sea whose ebb and flow*
> *At once is deaf and loud; and on the shore*
> *Vomits its wrecks, and still howls on for more*
> *Yet in its depth what treasures!*”
>
> **Percy Bysshe Shelley (1792–1822)**

Based on the private collection of the textiles magnate **Samuel Courtauld** (1876–1947), this is one art gallery which will leave you feeling refreshed rather than exhausted. An hour or two is enough to get to know the collection in detail and even to pick out a few favourites for in-depth study.

Among the older pieces on display are a 15th-century Flemish triptych by the **Master of Flémalle**, **Lucas Cranach**'s *Adam and Eve*, oil sketches by **Tiepolo** and several paintings by **Rubens**, including his contemplative *Moonlight Landscape*. The real attraction, though, is the collection of Impressionist and Post-Impressionist painting, unrivalled anywhere in London. Here are some of the finest works by the leading figures of the **Impressionist movement**, including **Monet**, **Manet**, **Cézanne**, **Degas**, **Renoir** and **Toulouse-Lautrec**. Everyone will have their own favourites, but particular works to look out for include Manet's *Bar at the Folies-Bergère*, Cézanne's *The Card Players* and Van Gogh's *Self-portrait with Bandaged Ear*. Renoir's *La Loge*, a portrait of a couple at the opera, was one of the first ever Impressionist paintings, created for the inaugural Impressionist exhibition in Paris in 1874. Years later, **Modigliani**'s *Female Nude* caused outrage when it was shown in Paris; although it is still extremely sensual, it has largely lost its power to shock.

Also in Somerset House, the **Gilbert Collection** (*opens May 2000; tel: (020) 7240 4080; open same hours and prices as Courtauld Gallery*), housed in the Embankment Buildings, is the result of a bequest from a London-born American property millionaire, **Sir Arthur Gilbert**, who left his entire decorative arts collection to the British people. The collection includes porcelain, furniture, clocks and miniature portraits, but the real treasures are the Italian mosaics, European silver and the set of gold snuff boxes made for **Frederick the Great of Prussia**.

Covent Garden

Leave aside the modern shops selling aromatherapy oils and designer clothes and you could still be in Dickensian London. Gypsies accost you with flowers, the smell of roasted chestnuts hangs in the air.

Covent Garden has its origins in the 'convent garden' of the Benedictine monastery that once stood on this site. The square that you see today was laid out in the 1630s by the King's Surveyor, **Inigo Jones**. This was London's first public square, modelled on the Renaissance squares that Jones had seen in Italy. When his client, the **Duke of Bedford**, asked for a 'barn' for a church, Jones is said to have replied: 'You shall have the handsomest barn in England'. The result is nearby **St Paul's Church**, a simple, classical-style temple with a barn-like portico. It was here in 1662 that **Samuel Pepys** witnessed the first **Punch and Judy** show ever recorded in England and the church porch is still used as the venue for entertainers from musicians to jugglers, fire-eaters to clowns. St Paul's is known as 'the actors' church' on account of its many connections with the nearby theatres.

A market licence was first granted in 1670 and the current buildings date from 1830, though the Victorian glass canopy was added later. For most of the 19th and 20th centuries this was London's main **fruit and vegetable market**, a hive of activity each morning. The market moved in 1974, to

be replaced in 1980 by the piazza, a continental-style bazaar of cafés and craft stalls which continues to perform its historic function as a bustling, central meeting-place.

Take a walk through the old **Apple Market**, where artists sell jewellery, paintings and handmade toys from the original apple carts. The avenues are given over to speciality shops, a few of them high-street names but mostly wacky, one-off outlets selling candles, lace or snuff. Old-fashioned toys and theatrical puppets are on sale at **Benjamin Pollock's Toy Shop**; children also enjoy the **Cabaret Mechanical Theatre**, with its museum collection of wonderful old fairground machines.

On the corner of the piazza, an entrance gives access to the **Royal Opera House** (*open: Mon–Sat 1000–1500*), reopened in 1999 after a controversial £214-million makeover. Although Londoners continue to complain about the cost, most have been won over by the sheer brilliance of the restoration. The Corinthian façade on Bow Street is once again glistening white and the Victorian glass-and-iron **Floral Hall** has been brought back to life as a magnificent foyer. As part of a new commitment to public access, the opera house is now open during the daytime; there is a rooftop restaurant and a terrace café with views over the piazza. Free lunchtime concerts are held in the Floral Hall, backstage tours are available and opera is brought to the masses through cheap tickets and live relays to the piazza outside.

Away from the piazza, Neal Street leads to **Neal's Yard**, a peaceful hippy haven of wholefood cafés, alternative therapists and potted plants. Just the place to enjoy a stress-relieving backrub or pick up an organic salad and a vegan loaf.

Getting there: Underground: Covent Garden or Leicester Square. Most shops are open Mon–Sat from around 1000–1800 and 1200–1700 on Sundays.

Inns of Court

Hidden away between Westminster and the City, the Inns of Court form the historic heartland of England's legal system.

Established in the 14th century to provide accommodation for lawyers and their students, they were closely modelled on the colleges of Oxford and Cambridge universities, with their courtyards, chapels, libraries and dining halls. Past students have included **Oliver Cromwell**, **Sir Walter Raleigh** and **Mahatma Gandhi**. **Charles Dickens** worked as a clerk at Gray's Inn and set the opening chapter of *Bleak House* in Lincoln's Inn Hall. Among recent prime ministers, **Margaret Thatcher** and **Tony Blair** both studied at Lincoln's Inn and Blair's wife, Cherie Booth, has 'chambers' in Gray's Inn Square. Even today, every practising barrister in England must be a member of one of the four Inns and eat a required number of dinners before being 'called to the Bar'.

The Inns are private institutions and the buildings are usually closed to the public, but you are welcome to stroll around the grounds – though watch out for stern notices prohibiting everything from dogs and bicycles to 'committing a nuisance'. You could start at **Gray's Inn**, entering through the 17th-century gatehouse from High Holborn and passing into South Square, where there is a bronze statue of the Inn's most illustrious former member, the philosopher and statesman **Sir Francis Bacon** (1561–1626). Bacon had a hand in laying out the gardens here, much beloved of Samuel Pepys as a good place in which to 'espy fine ladies'.

Lincoln's Inn also has attractive gardens, as well as the 17th-century chapel where the poet **John Donne** used to preach. The chapel bell rings out whenever a judge has died, the inspiration for Donne's famous line: 'Never send to know for whom the bell tolls; it tolls for thee'. Nearby, Lincoln's Inn Fields is the largest square in London. Among notable buildings on the square are **Sir John Soane's Museum** (*see page 101*) and the offices of **Farrows**, the Queen's solicitors, at No 66.

The final two Inns, **Inner Temple** and **Middle Temple**, are situated in an area known as the Temple on the south side of the Strand. With its bewigged barristers and gaslit lanes, this is legal London at its most atmospheric. The area takes its name from the **Knights Templar**, a 12th-century order of Crusaders, who built their round church here in 1185. The church, in transitional Romanesque and Gothic styles, was modelled on the Church of the Holy Sepulchre in Jerusalem. Look out for the remarkable effigies of medieval knights in armour on the floor of the nave. Not far from here, Middle Temple Hall is a 16th-century building with a fine hammerbeam roof. According to tradition, **Shakespeare** performed here for **Elizabeth I** at the premiere of *Twelfth Night* in 1602.

Temple Bar, where Fleet Street meets the Strand, is the historic dividing line between the cities of London and Westminster. The monarch must still stop here to receive permission of the Lord Mayor before entering the City. Near here, the **Royal Courts of Justice** (*open: Mon–Fri 0900–1630*) are where civil trials and appeals are heard; the public is admitted to the viewing galleries, but security is tight and cameras are not allowed inside the building. If you want to see a criminal trial, walk up Fleet Street and cross Ludgate Circus to reach the **Central Criminal Court**, commonly known as the 'Old Bailey'.

Getting there: Underground: Chancery Lane, Holborn or Temple.

National Gallery

Trafalgar Square. Tel: (020) 7747 2885; www.nationalgallery.org.uk. Underground: Charing Cross or Leicester Square. Open: 1000–1800 daily (Wed 1000–2100); closed Good Fri, 24–26 Dec and 1 Jan. £.

The National Gallery contains the national collection of West European art from the 13th to early 20th centuries. It was established in 1824 when Parliament set aside £57,000 to purchase the house and paintings of the late **John Julius Angerstein**, including works by **Rembrandt**, **Rubens** and **Titian**. Originally based in Angerstein's house in Pall Mall, the gallery moved to its present home in 1838, when **William Wilkins** completed his neo-classical design facing Trafalgar Square. A second building, the **Sainsbury Wing**, was added in 1991 after much public debate; at one stage the **Prince of Wales** derided earlier plans as 'a monstrous carbuncle on the face of a much-loved friend'. The eventual Post-Modern classical design met with his approval and is widely thought to complement the original, both in its style and in its use of Portland stone.

The collection has grown to more than 2,000 works of art and a visit can be exhausting. Put aside any thoughts of seeing everything in one visit. A good start is to take one of the regular free guided tours (*1130 and 1430 daily; also Wed*

1830), led by the gallery's art experts. These do not attempt to show you the 'highlights', but focus in depth on five or six paintings, chosen as a representative sample from the collection. Another option, made possible by the free admission policy, is to go several times, concentrating on a few rooms at a time. The collection is **arranged chronologically**, so it is relatively easy to pick out the works of a particular artist or genre. If you want to do more than just look, a free CD soundtrack has commentaries on almost every painting in the collection.

The oldest works, from the 13th to 15th centuries, are housed in the Sainsbury Wing. Among the artists featured here are **Leonardo da Vinci**, **Botticelli**, **Raphael** and **Bellini**. The building itself is a work of art, with doorways carved in grey *petra serena* (the stone of the Italian Renaissance) and paintings dramatically framed by a series of uneven arches that lend stunning and unexpected vistas. Masterpieces on show include the **Wilton Diptych** (*c* 1395), showing Richard II being presented to the Virgin and Child, and **Piero della Francesca**'s *Baptism of Christ.*

The main building is divided into three further wings. The West Wing features works from the 16th century by **Holbein**, **El Greco**, **Michelangelo**, **Tintoretto** and **Titian**. The North Wing is devoted to 17th-century art, with paintings by **Rubens** and **Rembrandt**, including a Rembrandt self-portrait. The most modern work, from the 18th and 19th centuries, is housed in the East Wing. Here, in Room 34, are **Constable's *The Haywain*** and **Turner's *Rain, Steam and Speed***, two of the few British paintings to be held at the National Gallery rather than at Tate Britain (*see page 47*). Finally, the Impressionist galleries are always popular, with works by **Renoir**, **Monet**, **Seurat**, **Van Gogh** and **Cézanne**. Among the paintings to look out for are Monet's *The Thames Below Westminster*, Renoir's *Boating on the Seine*, Seurat's *Bathers at Asnière* and a version of Van Gogh's *Sunflowers*.

Tip

From the terrace outside the main entrance there are superb views over Trafalgar Square and along Whitehall to Big Ben.

National Portrait Gallery

St Martin's Place. Tel: (020) 7306 0055; www.npg.org.uk. Underground: Charing Cross or Leicester Square. Open: Mon–Sat 1000–1800; Sun 1200–1800; closed Good Fri, 24–26 Dec and 1 Jan. £.

If your eyes glaze over while reading history textbooks and you struggle to make sense of all the various kings and queens, a visit here can bring history to life. Founded in 1856 to show portraits of distinguished men and women from British history, the National Portrait Gallery acts as a

historical 'Who's Who', covering the period from Tudor times to the present day. After a recent restoration the galleries are more visitor-friendly than ever, with a rooftop restaurant and huge picture window giving views of the London skyline across Trafalgar Square.

The first item to be acquired by the collection was a portrait of **William Shakespeare** by an unknown artist, the only known contemporary portrait of England's great Elizabethan playwright. Other early portraits, housed in the Tudor Gallery, include **Holbein**'s full-length cartoon of **Henry VIII** and a portrait of **Elizabeth I** by Marcus Gheeraerts the Younger, which shows 'the Virgin Queen' standing in triumph on a map of England.

The increasing democratisation of British life is clear as you move through the collection, as monarchs and their courtiers gradually give way to artists, scientists and figures from popular culture. Until the 1960s, no portraits of living people were shown, but these days you can find such well-known names as the footballer **Bobby Charlton**, the songwriter **Paul McCartney** and former prime ministers **John Major** and **Margaret Thatcher**. Among recent royal portraits commissioned for the gallery are **Diana, Princess of Wales** by Bryan Organ and an enigmatic, pained portrait of **Prince Charles** by Tom Wood.

Sir John Soane's Museum

13 Lincoln's Inn Fields. Underground: Holborn. Tel: (020) 7430 0175. Open: Tue–Sat 1000–1700 (also first Tuesday of every month, 1800–2100). Guided tours: Sat 1430 (these are deservedly popular and you should arrive well before tickets go on sale at 1400 in order to obtain one of the 25 places). £.

This group of houses was bequeathed to the nation by **Sir John Soane** (1753–1837), the son of a bricklayer who went on to design the Bank of England and become the greatest architect of his day. Soane has recently undergone something of a revival in fashion and a visit to this museum gives fascinating insights into his mind. The house in which he lived is laid out just as he designed it, a labyrinth of rooms filled with antiquities, with cleverly concealed mirrors creating a teasing interplay of light, colour and glass.

Soane was an avid collector of everything from **Etruscan vases** to furniture and books and the best way to approach the museum is to wander around the house making chance discoveries. There are, however, a couple of items that must be seen. In the crypt, modelled on ancient catacombs, is the **sarcophagus of Seti I**, the Egyptian pharaoh who died around 1300 BC. This is one of the most important Egyptian discoveries ever made. Upstairs in the Picture Room, where the walls open to reveal more and more paintings, are two series of sketches by **William Hogarth**. *The Rake's Progress* tells the story of a dissolute young man's downfall as he squanders his fortune on gambling and women, while *The Election* is a brilliant satire on bribery and corruption, almost as relevant today as when it was painted in 1754.

Theatre Museum

Russell Street. Underground: Covent Garden. Tel: (020) 7836 7891. Open: Tue–Sun 1000–1800. ££.

Situated at the heart of London's theatreland, a few steps away from the oldest West End theatre, is Britain's national museum of the performing arts. It is not just theatre that is represented, but the whole variety of 'the stage', from music hall to pantomime, opera, ballet and burlesque. A series of display cases covers the history of British theatre since Shakespeare, featuring playbills, programmes, props, costumes and personal items such as **Noel Coward**'s monogrammed dressing gown and slippers. More interesting for children are the interactive sections of the museum, with make-up and costume workshops taking place daily. Look out too for special exhibitions and for the **Wall of Fame**, a long gallery of coloured handprints created by actors such as **Sir John Gielgud** and **Dame Peggy Ashcroft**.

Around the corner in Catherine Street, the **Theatre Royal Drury Lane** first opened in 1663 as one of only two theatres in London licensed to stage plays. **Charles II** was a frequent visitor and it was here that he first met 'pretty witty Nell', the orange-seller **Nell Gwyn**, who later became an actress as well as the king's mistress. According to tradition, it was during performances at the Theatre Royal that Charles would slip across the road to meet Nell in an upstairs room at the local tavern, now a cosy pub by the name of Old Nell at the Drury. The current theatre, used for lavish musical productions, is actually the fourth on this site. The first burnt down in 1674 and was rebuilt by Sir Christopher Wren.

London Transport Museum

Covent Garden Piazza. Tel: (020) 7379 6344; www.ltmuseum.co.uk. Underground: Covent Garden. Open: Sat–Thur 1000–1800; Fri 1100–1800; closed 24–26 Dec. ££.

This museum, housed in the old Covent Garden flower market, is just the place to take the children on a rainy day. Small boys in particular seem to love clambering over the **old buses and trams**, while adults will grow nostalgic looking at the posters, bus maps and vehicles of their childhood. Although the vehicles themselves are the main attraction, there are enough hands-on exhibits and interactive displays to keep even the most restless children happy, as they take turns at driving the underground train simulator or work out why trams are more efficient than buses.

The story of London's transport is one that is worth telling. It begins in 1829, with a replica of the very first omnibus, a **horse-drawn bus** service that ran from Paddington to Bank with a fixed fare of one shilling (five pence). Buses gave way to trams, and trams to trolleybuses, and in 1863 the world's first underground train line opened in London. At weekends and during school holidays, actors in Victorian costume bring this period to life as they show how tunnels were dug beneath the streets and **steam engines** were eventually replaced by electric trains. The displays are brought up to date with the formation of London Transport in 1933, the development of the **Routemaster bus** (still considered a 20th-century design classic), the arrival of the **Docklands Light Railway** and a look into London's transport options for the future. One sobering statistic to ponder as you walk around is that the average speed of the traffic on central London's streets is no faster today than it was in the age of the horse-drawn tram.

Shopping

Around Covent Garden

The old market buildings have been taken over by a mix of high-street chains, offbeat fashions and small, quirky shops. One shop not to be missed is **Lush**, which features cosmetics made out of natural ingredients ranging from fresh fruit to wild rice. Soap is piled high in wedges the size of cheeses, giving Lush the look and feel of a high-class delicatessen.

The shops around the piazza are mostly unexceptional, but **Dr Martens Dept Store** (*1–4 King Street*) has five floors of the sturdy footwear that has become an icon of British youth culture. In nearby Floral Street, an enclave of men's fashion, the leading British designer **Paul Smith** (*40–4 Floral Street*) has accessories for men, women and kids.

Away from the piazza, Neal Street is lined with unusual, slightly alternative shops. **Neal Street East** (*No 5*) is an Aladdin's cave of Oriental fashions, crafts and jewellery, from Indian textiles to Chinese jade. **The Tea House** (*No 15A*) sells everything for tea lovers, while the **Natural Shoe Store** (*No 21*) has wooden-soled 'vegetarian' sandals. **Neal's Yard Dairy** (*17 Shorts Gardens*) is the smelliest shop in London, piled high with British and Irish farmhouse cheeses and breads from the bakery around the back.

Pubs

The Devereux (*Devereux Court*) is a former coffee house among the gaslit lanes of the Temple, now a pub serving standard English fare. Not far from here, **Ye Olde Cheshire Cheese** (*145 Fleet Street*) is one of London's oldest pubs, a haunt of **Dr Johnson** whose chair still stands here. With its snugs and timber-framed bars, this has become something of a tourist trap but is still worth a visit. Around Covent Garden, the **Lamb & Flag** (*33 Rose Street*) is as British as they come, while the **Coach & Horses** (*42 Wellington Street*) is a genuine Irish pub with real Guinness and huge roast beef sandwiches.

Restaurants

Bank

1 Kingsway. Tel: (020) 7379 9797. ££. The latest mega-restaurant from design guru **Terence Conran** serves up modern European fusion cuisine as well as caviar, champagne and hearty English breakfasts.

Belgo Centraal

50 Earlham Street. Tel: (020) 7813 2233. £. This ultra-modern Belgian bistro has taken Covent Garden by storm. The house speciality is a kilo pot of mussels with chips, but you can also have wild boar sausages, Belgian chocolate ice-cream and beer served by waiters attired as **Trappist monks**.

Calabash

38 King Street. Tel: (020) 7836 1976. £. Located in the basement of the Africa Centre, this restaurant features dishes from several countries of **Africa**, such as chicken in peanut sauce and spicy lentils with *injera* (Ethiopian bread). The attached bar often has live Afro-Caribbean bands.

Chez Gérard at the Opera Terrace

Covent Garden Piazza. Tel: (020) 7379 0666. ££. Steak with *frites* is the thing to order at this popular French bistro, with an outdoor terrace in summer overlooking the piazza and the Royal Opera House.

Neal Street

26 Neal Street. Tel: (020) 7836 8368. ££. Celebrity chef **Antonio Carluccio** turns out classic Italian cooking, with an emphasis on the use of wild mushrooms and truffles. The delicatessen next door has a good selection of pastas, oils and Italian cheese.

Rules

35 Maiden Lane. Tel: (020) 7836 5314. ££. First opened as an oyster bar in 1798, the customers at London's oldest restaurant have included **Charles Dickens** and **Edward VII**. The food is traditional English, featuring game in season from the restaurant's own Pennine estate.

J Sheekey

28–32 St Martin's Court. Tel: (020) 7240 2565. ££. This old fish and chip restaurant has been thoroughly transformed and now turns out inspired **fish** dishes, both traditional and modern, to theatregoers, in a succession of wood-panelled, stained-glass rooms.

Simpsons-in-the-Strand

100 Strand. Tel: (020) 7836 9112. ££. This deeply traditional restaurant, reminiscent of a gentlemen's club, specialises in old English fare, with roast beef carved from a trolley at your table and served up with overcooked vegetables. Men must wear a jacket and tie and jeans are not allowed.

World Food Café

14 Neal's Yard. Tel: (020) 7379 0298. £. Of several vegetarian eateries in Neal's Yard, this place really stands out. Chris and Carolyn Caldicott collect recipes on their travels and produce delicious healthy dishes inspired by the cuisine of India, Sri Lanka, West Africa, Mexico and Turkey.

Trafalgar Square

Trafalgar Square is London's central square. This is where Londoners come to protest, to celebrate, to feed the pigeons and clamber over the lions at the foot of Nelson's Column. It is where, each December, carols are sung beneath an enormous Norwegian Christmas tree and crowds of drunken revellers see in the New Year while listening to the chimes of Big Ben.

Like the city it symbolises, Trafalgar Square has never really been planned but has grown haphazardly into a strangely harmonious whole. The present square owes most to **John Nash**, who designed the basic layout in 1820, and **Charles Barry**, architect of the Houses of Parliament, who completed the square in 1840. **Nelson's Column**, perhaps London's best-loved monument, was erected in 1843 in honour of Lord Nelson, who lost his life defeating **Napoleon** at the Battle of Trafalgar. The famous bronze lions, by **Sir Edwin Landseer**, were added to the base of the column in 1867, while the fountains by **Sir Edwin Lutyens** are a 20th-century addition.

Of the many monuments to admirals, generals and kings, the most interesting is the equestrian statue of **Charles I**, which stands on a traffic island at the head of Whitehall. Cast by **Hubert Le Sueur** in 1633,

> *I thought of London spread out in the sun*
> *Its postal districts packed like squares of wheat.*

Philip Larkin, *The Whitsun Weddings*, 1964

the statue was ordered to be destroyed by **Oliver Cromwell** but was secretly hidden and re-erected during the reign of **Charles II**. Members of the Royal Stuart Society, supporters of Charles I, still gather here on 30 January each year to lay wreaths in honour of the beheaded king. The statue stands on the site of the original **Charing Cross**, the point from which all distances to London are measured.

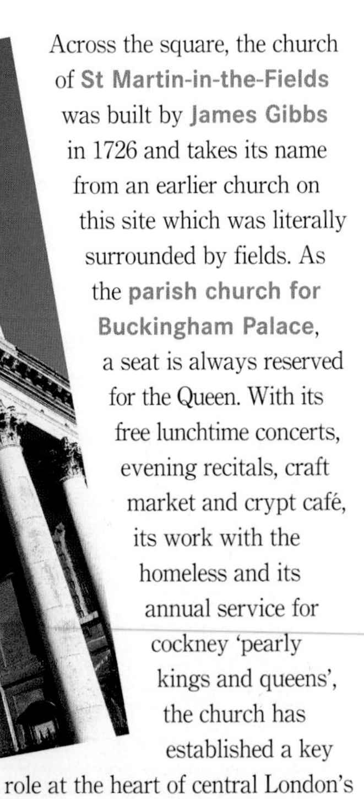

Across the square, the church of **St Martin-in-the-Fields** was built by **James Gibbs** in 1726 and takes its name from an earlier church on this site which was literally surrounded by fields. As the **parish church for Buckingham Palace**, a seat is always reserved for the Queen. With its free lunchtime concerts, evening recitals, craft market and crypt café, its work with the homeless and its annual service for cockney 'pearly kings and queens', the church has established a key role at the heart of central London's community life. Behind the church, a modern statue of **Oscar Wilde** is engraved with his memorable words: 'We are all in the gutter, but some of us are looking at the stars'.

The City

Though the City of London, known as the* Square Mile, *is a global financial centre, it is also where London best preserves its medieval street pattern and some of its most cherished traditions.

The City

Getting there: the most useful ***underground*** *stations are Bank and St Paul's, plus Tower Hill for Tower Bridge, the Tower of London and St Katharine's Dock. As a busy commuter district, the City is ringed by underground stations, including Barbican, Farringdon, Blackfriars, Mansion House, Cannon Street, Monument, Liverpool Street and Moorgate – all of which can be reached on the Circle Line.*

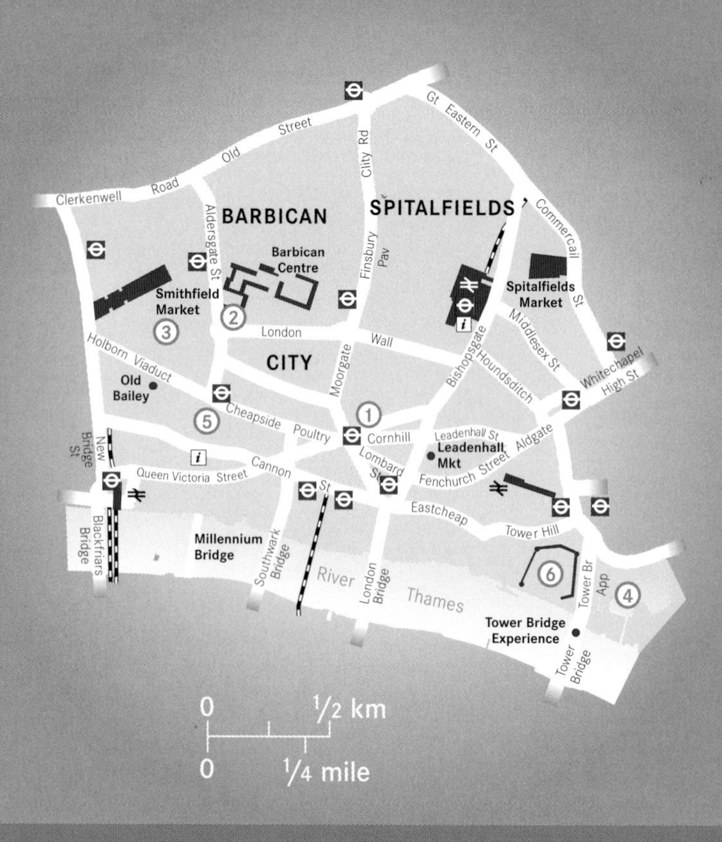

① Bank of England Museum

This fascinating museum traces the **history of money** and the City's role as a centre of financial trading, with exhibits ranging from banknotes to gold bars. Budding capitalists will love it here. Page 112

② Museum of London

The largest city museum in the world takes a provocative look at **London's history**, from prehistoric and Roman times to poll tax riots and tower blocks. Interactive exhibits and model Victorian sweet shops help to keep younger visitors amused. Page 113

③ St Bartholomew-the-Great

London's oldest surviving church was founded in the 12th century on the edge of the 'smooth field', a medieval market and execution ground. Smithfield market now stands on the border between the City and the artists' village of Clerkenwell. Pages 120–1

④ St Katharine's Dock

Historic vessels are moored alongside luxury yachts at this **charming marina**, built on the site of the former commercial docks. With its waterfront restaurants and concerts on the quayside, this is a great place for a stroll on a summer afternoon.
Page 119

⑤ St Paul's Cathedral

Sir Christopher Wren's masterpiece, built out of the ruins of the Great Fire, dominates the London skyline. If you have the energy, climb up to the dome for panoramic views of the City.
Pages 114–15

⑥ Tower of London

'**Beefeaters**' in Tudor costume regale visitors to this ancient fortress with tales of its long and bloody history, including the executions of two of Henry VIII's six wives. Among the treasures on display are the **Crown Jewels**, still used at coronations and state occasions. Pages 116–17

Tourist information

The City of London has its own tourist office, located opposite the south side of St Paul's Cathedral. *St Paul's Churchyard. Tel: (020) 7332 1456. Open: Apr–Sept, 0930–1700 daily; Oct–Mar, Mon–Fri 0930–1700, Sat 0930–1230.*

Tip

Although some 250,000 commuters travel into the City during the week, fewer than 6,000 people live here. As a result, the same streets that are a hive of activity from Monday to Friday become deserted and hauntingly atmospheric at weekends.

Bank of England

Threadneedle Street. Underground: Bank. Tel: (020) 7601 5545.

The Bank of England was established by Royal Charter in 1694 in order to finance a war against France. It moved to its present premises in 1734, giving rise to its nickname 'the Old Lady of Threadneedle Street'. The current building, designed by **Sir John Soane** (*see page 101*), features the huge, rock-solid, windowless outer walls, a symbol of the Bank's role as protector of the British economy.

Soane's Stock Office has been carefully rebuilt to serve as the entrance hall of the **Bank of England Museum** (*entrance in Bartholomew Lane; open: Mon–Fri 1000–1700; £*). The museum follows the history of the Bank from its foundation to its nationalisation in 1946 and privatisation by the Labour government in 1997. The exhibits include letters from past customers, among them George Washington, and a comprehensive collection of British banknotes beginning with handwritten 17th-century receipts. A display case holds 59 facsimile gold bars which, if they were genuine, would be worth over £72,000 each.

The surrounding area, simply known as Bank, contains several interesting buildings. The 15th-century **Guildhall**, historic meeting-place of the medieval trade guilds, is where the City's local government meets, with figures of Gog and Magog, mythical founders of Britain, looking on from the gallery. You can visit the Guildhall when it is not in use. **Mansion House** is the home of the Lord Mayor, elected each year by the City guilds. On the second Saturday in November, the new Lord Mayor proceeds from the Guildhall to the Royal Courts of Justice in a gilded state coach, leading a colourful parade of liveried floats. The Lord Mayor's coach is one of the exhibits in the Museum of London (*see opposite*).

Museum of London

London Wall. Tel: (020) 7600 3699; www.museumoflondon.org.uk. Underground: Barbican or St Paul's. Open: Mon–Sat 1000–1750; Sun 1200–1750. ££ (free after 1630).

Do not be put off by the dreary 1970s exterior of this museum, above a busy roundabout on the edge of the Barbican complex. The museum covers the history of London in an interactive and challenging way, dealing with such issues as gender and multiculturalism and their role in the city's history. The exhibits are arranged chronologically, beginning with **prehistoric London** and the arrival of the Romans, who laid the foundations of the modern city when they built their first bridge over the Thames. There are views down over a section of the 2nd-century Roman wall and fragments from the **Temple of Mithras**, whose ruins still stand in Queen Victoria Street.

> " *I love this concrete jungle still*
> *With all its sirens and its speed*
> *The people here united will*
> *Create a kind of London breed.* "
>
> **Benjamin Zephaniah, *The London Breed***

The section on **medieval London** includes a scale model of the old St Paul's cathedral, completed in 1327 and destroyed in the Great Fire. The fire itself is covered in the **Fire Experience**, an audiovisual model of London burning accompanied by extracts from the diary of Samuel Pepys. Most visitors are captivated by the more recent aspects of London's history, from suffragettes and department stores to red telephone boxes, the Swinging Sixties and the phenomenon of Cool Britannia. A thoughtful exhibition called **London Now** ends with a poem by the rap artist Benjamin Zephaniah (*see above*).

St Paul's Cathedral

Ludgate Hill. Underground: Blackfriars, Mansion House or St Paul's. Tel: (020) 7236 4128. Open: Mon–Sat 0830–1600. Closed on Sundays except for services. Free.

The magnificent lead dome of St Paul's, floodlit at night, is the defining feature of the City skyline. The cathedral has had a special place in Londoners' affections ever since the **Second World War**, when it miraculously survived the bombs of the Blitz. No one who sees it will ever forget the iconic image of the dome wreathed in smoke while buildings burned all around.

Tip

To hear the famous St Paul's choir, go to Evensong (Mon–Sat 1700, Sun 1515) or to the weekly Sung Eucharist (Sun 1130).

The image was so powerful because it recalled the cathedral's origins, born out of the ruins of the **Great Fire of 1666**. A church had stood on this site since AD 604 and a great Norman cathedral since the 12th century. **Sir Christopher Wren** had already been commissioned to restore the cathedral when it burned down, giving him the opportunity to create his masterpiece. Built after the Reformation, this was the first purpose-built Protestant church in Europe, England's only baroque cathedral and the only one with a dome. Wren himself is buried in the crypt. Beneath the dome, an inscription in the pavement, composed by his son, reads *Si monumentum requiris, circumspice* ('If you seek his monument, look around you') – a handsome and fitting tribute.

Before you go in, stand back on Ludgate Hill to admire the west front. The cathedral is so hemmed in by buildings that this is one of the few genuine vistas, along with the splendid new approach from the Millennium footbridge across the Thames. Once you have entered, look down the nave to experience the cathedral's full extent. This has been the setting for numerous great events, including the **funerals of Lord Nelson and Winston Churchill** and the **wedding of Prince Charles to Lady Diana Spencer** in 1981.

> *Sir Christopher Wren*
> *Said, 'I am going to dine with some men.*
> *If anybody calls*
> *Say I am designing St Paul's'.*

E Clerihew Bentley, *Biography for Beginners*, 1905

After this, it is best to follow the recommended route described on the leaflet given to visitors. Passing monuments to military heroes such as **General Gordon** and the **Duke of Wellington**, look out for **Holman Hunt**'s painting *Light of the World* in the north transept. The tour continues past the choir and main altar, richly decorated with mahogany, marble, mosaic and gold leaf. After passing the effigy of **John Donne**, the poet who became Dean of St Paul's, go down into the crypt, where numerous statesmen are buried, including Lord Nelson and the Duke of Wellington. Near Wren's tomb, **Painters' Corner** is the equivalent of Poets' Corner in Westminster Abbey, with monuments to **Constable**, **Turner**, **Reynolds**, **Millais** and **Van Dyck**. Others remembered in the crypt, a roll-call of English history, are the nurse **Florence Nightingale**, the chemist **Alexander Fleming** and the newspaper magnate **Lord Thomson of Fleet**.

The climax of any visit is a climb to the **dome** (an extra charge is payable). This is a steep climb up a long spiral staircase, but the reward is one of the best views in London. On the way, pause in the **Whispering Gallery** for views down over the nave and up to the frescos in the dome. Take care, as the acoustics in the circular gallery mean that your whispers will be picked up by people sitting on the far side.

In all, Sir Christopher Wren designed some 52 City churches to replace those destroyed in the Great Fire. One of them, **St Mary-le-Bow** on Cheapside, is the home of the 'Bow Bells', within the sound of which all true 'cockney' Londoners are born.

Tower Bridge

Underground: Tower Hill.

This splendid Victorian bridge is as famous for its profile as for its revolutionary engineering design. Completed in 1894 to ease traffic congestion across the river, its most remarkable feature is the bridge that lifts up to let tall ships pass beneath. The bridge is still raised about 500 times a year and makes an impressive sight.

The twin Gothic towers, made of steel frames encased in stone, contain the hydraulic machinery that enables the bridge to work. All this is explained in the **Tower Bridge Experience** (*tel: (020) 7626 2717; open: 1000–1800 daily; ££*), a mocked-up history of the bridge complete with videos, special effects and animatronic cockney characters. The tour gives access to the high-level walkways, with panoramic views over London and along the Thames. Afterwards, you can visit the original Victorian engine rooms, which powered the bridge by steam until 1976.

Tower of London

Tower Hill. Underground: Tower Hill. Riverboat services from Westminster, Embankment and Greenwich. Tel: (020) 7709 0765. Open: Mar–Oct, Mon–Sat 0900–1700, Sun 1000–1700; Nov–Feb, Mon–Sat 0900–1600, Sun 1000–1600. £££.

With its famously long queues and a reverence for quaint traditions (which sits uneasily with the city's Cool Britannia image), the Tower of London tends to be ignored by most

Londoners. This is a pity, as it is a genuinely historical building with a wealth of interesting sights and a key role in London's long and bloody history.

Begun by **William the Conqueror** around 1078, the Tower has served as a fortress, a royal residence, a prison and a place of execution. Among those to have been imprisoned, tortured or executed here are **Anne Boleyn** and **Catherine Howard**, two of Henry VIII's six wives; **Lady Jane Grey**, Queen for just nine days in 1553; and **Guy Fawkes**, the Catholic conspirator who tried to blow up the Houses of Parliament. Prisoners were brought to the Tower by boat through **Traitors' Gate**, after passing beneath London Bridge where the severed heads of execution victims were exhibited on spikes. **Bloody Tower**, beside Traitors' Gate, was where **Sir Walter Raleigh** was held prisoner and was also the setting for the murder of the 'little princes', **Edward V** and **Richard of York**, on the orders of their uncle **Richard III**. It is hardly surprising that the Tower is thought to be the most haunted building in London.

There is so much to see here that you should allow around half a day. A good way to get your bearings is to go on one of the regular free tours guided by '**Beefeaters**', Yeoman Warders in Tudor costume who have been guarding the Tower since 1485. If time is short, head for the **White Tower**, the original 11th-century keep with its fine Norman windows and arches; inside is the beautiful **Chapel of St John**, where medieval monarchs passed the night before their coronation. Another must-see is the **Jewel House**, where the famous **Crown Jewels** are kept. Among the treasures on display is the **world's largest diamond**, housed in the Royal Sceptre; the Koh-i-Noor diamond from India, set into the Queen Mother's crown; and the Imperial State Crown, made for Queen Victoria and worn by the Queen for the State Opening of Parliament each year.

Tip

You can avoid the worst of the queues by arriving early in the day, or buying your ticket in advance from any underground station. Fast-track entrance tickets to the Tower are also sold in combination with river cruises and open-top bus tours.

Restaurants and pubs

*Although there are numerous restaurants and wine bars in the Bank area frequented by City traders, the dining scene is gradually shifting north to trendy Smithfield and Clerkenwell (*see pages 120–1*). Most restaurants in the City are closed at weekends.*

Club Gascon
57 West Smithfield. Tel: (020) 7253 5853. ££. This sensational new arrival serves the food of southwest France in *tapas*-style portions. *Foie gras* features heavily, along with duck *confit* and *cassoulet*. The atmosphere is informal and there is a good range of French regional wines.

Coq d'Argent
1 Poultry. Tel: (020) 7395 5000. ££. Situated on the top floor of the City's most eye-catching piece of modern architecture, this stylish restaurant has an indoor roof garden and an outdoor terrace in summer. The food is traditional French, from *coq au vin* to *steak au poivre*.

Fox & Anchor
115 Charterhouse Street. Tel: (020) 7253 4838. £. This busy pub is the best place to try the legendary Smithfield breakfast, served to market porters from 0700 on weekdays. How about fried eggs, bacon, sausage, liver, kidneys, black pudding, mushrooms, tomato and fried bread, washed down with Guinness or champagne?

Gaudi
63 Clerkenwell Road. Tel: (020) 7608 3220. ££. One of London's top Spanish restaurants is found in a garage-like nightclub building in Clerkenwell, decorated with Catalan-style Modernist touches. For cheaper Spanish food, try **Las Brasas**, a *tapas* bar in the same building.

Jamaica Wine House
St Michael's Alley. Tel: (020) 7626 9496. Closed at weekends. £. This old-fashioned pub is found in one of the City's most atmospheric alleys on the site of London's first coffee house. There is food downstairs at lunchtimes and snacks in the bar, where port is a speciality.

The Place Below
St Mary-le-Bow, Cheapside. Tel: (020) 7329 0789. £. The best lunch deal in the City is this gourmet vegetarian restaurant in the crypt of Sir Christopher Wren's church, with tables outside in the churchyard in summer. Occasional lunchtime concerts are held in the church itself.

Quality Chop House
92–4 Farringdon Road. Tel: (020) 7837 5093. ££. The no-nonsense approach of this Edwardian dining-room, where the diners share wooden benches and the tables are laid with tomato ketchup and HP sauce, disguises one of London's finest British restaurants, featuring classics such as jellied eels or liver and bacon as well as dishes for the more sophisticated palate.

St John

26 St John Street. Tel: (020) 7251 0848. ££. Chef Fergus Henderson does all manner of things with **offal** in this stark-looking former smokehouse by Smithfield market. Try chitterlings with mash, bone marrow with parsley, pheasant and trotter pie, and for pudding, Lancashire cheese with Eccles cakes.

Simpsons Tavern

Ball Court, 38 1/2 Cornhill. Tel: (020) 7626 9985. £. This pub, which opened in 1757, may have been 'the usual melancholy tavern' fraternised by Charles Dickens' Scrooge. It continues to serve comfort food such as egg mayonnaise, roast dinners and steamed puddings to City types nostalgic for school dinners.

St Katharine's Dock

This former commercial dock, built by Thomas Telford in the early 19th century, has been redeveloped as London's premier marina, where historic vessels are moored beside luxury yachts. Office workers come here to relax in summer, when there is a programme of free concerts on the quayside. Among the dining options are **Aquarium** (*tel: (020) 7480 6116; ££*), a smart fish restaurant with a terrace overlooking the marina, and the **Dickens Inn** (*tel: (020) 7488 2208; £*), a timber-framed brewery dating back to 1740 which now serves everyday pub grub.

Shopping

***Leadenhall Market** is a handsome Victorian arcade, built on the site of London's oldest market in 1881. The market contains two wonderful, old-fashioned butcher's shops – **R S Ashby**, which specialises in Scotch beef and the aptly named **Butcher & Edmonds**, where game birds hang from butcher's hooks. Other gourmet food shops are the fishmongers **H S Linwood** and **Ashdown Oysters**, selling oysters, lobster and smoked salmon. Of several places to eat, the best is the original **Leadenhall Wine Bar**, which these days houses a tapas bar.*

City fringes

North and east of the City are a number of old villages, swallowed up by the expansion of 19th-century London. Historically, these villages have provided a home for refugees and outsiders, from French Huguenots to Jews and Bengalis. Even now, they retain a separate sense of identity and a nonconformism that sets them apart from the City and makes them fascinating to explore.

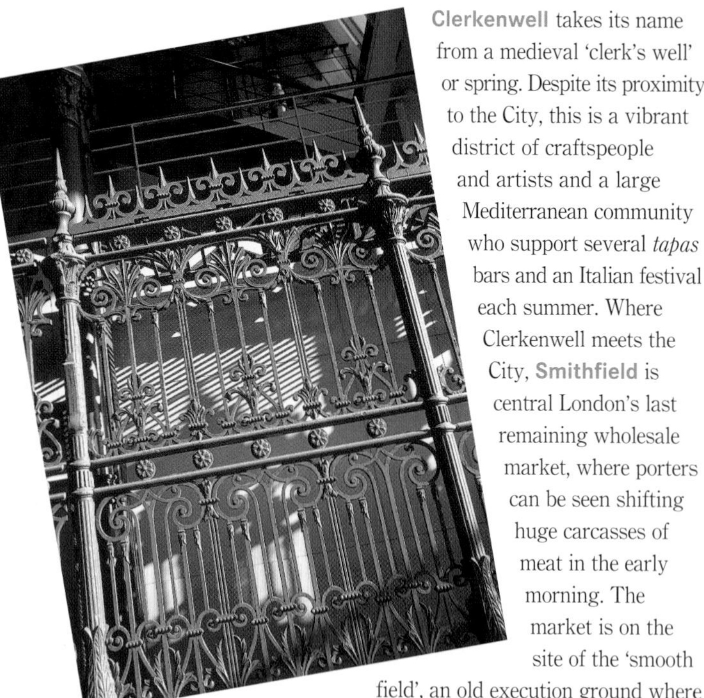

Clerkenwell takes its name from a medieval 'clerk's well' or spring. Despite its proximity to the City, this is a vibrant district of craftspeople and artists and a large Mediterranean community who support several *tapas* bars and an Italian festival each summer. Where Clerkenwell meets the City, **Smithfield** is central London's last remaining wholesale market, where porters can be seen shifting huge carcasses of meat in the early morning. The market is on the site of the 'smooth field', an old execution ground where the rebels **Wat Tyler** and **William Wallace** lost their heads. Near the market, look out for a timber-framed gateway leading to **St Bartholomew-the-Great**, London's

oldest surviving church. It was founded in 1123 by **Rahere**, **Henry I**'s court jester, at the same time as the neighbouring St Bartholomew's Hospital. Rahere is buried inside the church in a Gothic tomb. If the church looks familiar, it probably is – it has featured in several films, including *Four Weddings and a Funeral* and *Shakespeare in Love*.

The East End districts of **Spitalfields**, **Whitechapel** and **Bethnal Green** were once notorious for their **Dickensian slums**. It was here that **Jack the Ripper**, London's most infamous serial killer, murdered six prostitutes in 1888. It was here too that Jews established the rag trade, which still provides employment to many Bengali immigrants in sweatshops that differ little from their Victorian equivalents. **Brick Lane** in Spitalfields, at the heart of 'Banglatown', is the scene of one of London's most sprawling markets, which takes place on Sunday mornings (*0600–1300*) and almost merges with the more traditional Jewish and cockney market at nearby **Petticoat Lane** (*Middlesex Street*). Another attraction is the **Bethnal Green Museum of Childhood** (*Cambridge Heath Road; underground to Bethnal Green; tel: (020) 8983 5200; open: Sun–Thur 1000–1750; £*), which has a wonderful collection of historical toys, games, doll's houses and children's clothes.

" *London is a modern Babylon.* "

Benjamin Disraeli, 1847

THE SOUTH BANK

The South Bank

Traditionally the entertainment district, in contrast to the serious business of government and finance on the north side, this is now a vibrant area of new and enjoyable attractions, linked by the finest riverside walk in London.

The South Bank

Getting there: the best ***underground*** *stations are Waterloo, Southwark and London Bridge, though a pleasant alternative is to travel to Westminster, Embankment, Blackfriars, Monument or Tower Hill and cross one of the bridges to reach the South Bank. River piers at Festival (by Waterloo Bridge), Bankside, London Bridge City and Butler's Wharf have frequent* ***ferry*** *links to the north bank.*

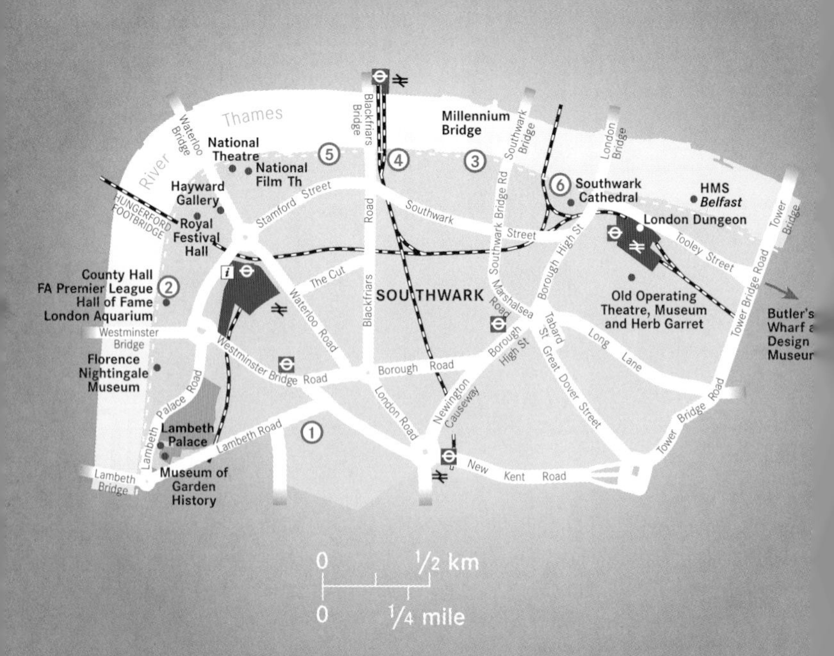

① *Imperial War Museum*

Despite its jingoistic name, far from glorifying war this museum takes a thoughtful look at the horrors of modern warfare, seen through the major conflicts of the 20th century. The museum also has a fine collection of planes, tanks and submarines. **Page 128**

② *London Eye*

The largest observation wheel in the world has transformed the London skyline and given Londoners a new vantage point from which to enjoy their city. You can love it or hate it, but you cannot ignore it. **Page 129**

③ *Shakespeare's Globe*

The first thatched building in London for more than 300 years is this reconstruction of a Shakespearean theatre, where plays are performed in the open air just as they were in Elizabethan times. **Page 131**

④ *Tate Modern*

The national collection of modern art has been given a stunning new home in this disused power station, flooded with natural light. A stylish new footbridge connects the Tate at Bankside with St Paul's Cathedral on the north bank. **Pages 132–3**

⑤ *Thames Path*

This riverside walk follows the Thames from its source in the Cotswolds to the sea. The stretch between Lambeth and Tower Bridges has some of the finest views in London and is particularly special at night when the embankments are lit up. **Pages 136–7**

⑥ *Vinopolis*

London's latest themed attraction for adults is this enjoyable wine odyssey, a high-tech journey through the world of wine with the opportunity to sample everything from port to vintage champagne. **Page 133**

Tourist information

The Southwark Information Centre near London Bridge is a good source of information and books about this up-and-coming district. *6 Tooley Street. Tel: (020) 7403 8299. Open: Easter–Oct, Mon–Sat 1000–1800, Sun 1030–1730; Nov–Easter, Mon–Sat 1000–1600, Sun 1100–1600.*

Tip

Don't miss the Saturday food market at Borough Market, near Southwark Cathedral and London Bridge, a good place to buy top-quality farmhouse foods from all over Britain. The biggest market takes place on the third Saturday of each month (see page 134 ***).***

Butler's Wharf

Underground: Bermondsey or London Bridge. Riverboat to London Bridge City or Butler's Wharf.

Nothing illustrates the changes on London's riverbanks more dramatically than the transformation of the city's waterfront districts since the closure of the docks in the 1960s. During the Victorian era, this area was known as 'the capital of cholera', a dark and dangerous district of prostitutes, ragged children and overflowing sewers, the inspiration for Bill Sykes' criminal lair in Charles Dickens' novel *Oliver Twist*. Now the area between Bankside and Bermondsey has a new name, **London Bridge City**, more in tune with the aspirations of the '**yuppies**' (young urban professionals) who were attracted to move here in the 1980s and 1990s. Butler's Wharf was the first modern docklands development when it was begun in 1984, blazing a trail that has changed the face of the capital from Bermondsey to Greenwich.

Butler's Wharf was the brainchild of **Sir Terence Conran**, style guru and founder of the Habitat chain of shops, who took the wharves and warehouses where coffee and spices were once stored and turned them into luxury apartments and shops. The restaurants on the quayside (*see page 135*) have become some of the most fashionable in London, a favourite haunt of rich young executives who want to impress their friends. Behind the waterfront, **Shad Thames** is a narrow street lined with sheer warehouse walls and high-level metal gangways once used by barrow boys to transport goods from the docks. Unlike some of the newer riverside housing developments, the entire scheme is sympathetic to the area's history and architecture.

Conran's **Design Museum** (*28 Shad Thames; tel: (020) 7378 6055; open: 1130–1800 daily; ££*) opened in 1989 in a restored 1950s warehouse. As the world's only museum devoted to 20th-century design, it features classic models such as early television sets, the Belling electric cooker and Hoover's first automatic washing machine, as well as typewriters, cameras, Coke bottles and hamburger cartons, and a provocative series of changing exhibitions.

HMS *Belfast*

Underground: London Bridge. Riverboat to London Bridge City. Tel: (020) 7940 6300. Open: Mar–Oct, 1000–1800 daily; Nov–Feb, 1000–1700 daily. ££ (children free).

HMS *Belfast* is the last of the big gun armoured warships that saw service during the Second World War. Launched in 1938 and almost destroyed by a German mine the following year, she played a leading part in the Battle of North Cape and the D-Day **Normandy Landings**. After serving with **United Nations** forces in Korea, she was saved from the scrap-yard in 1971 and is now run as an outpost of the Imperial War Museum. Children in particular enjoy the freedom to explore the ship, from the quarterdeck to the bridge, and down through nine decks to the boiler rooms. As you scramble up and down the steep, narrow ladders to reach the sailors' cabins, you get a feel for the cramped and difficult conditions of life in the Royal Navy.

“A town such as London, where a man may wander for hours without reaching the beginning of the end … this colossal centralisation, this heaping together of two and a half million human beings, has raised London to the commercial capital of the world, created the giant docks and assembled the thousand vessels that continually cover the Thames.”

Friedrich Engels, *The Conditions of the Working Class in England*, 1844

Imperial War Museum

Lambeth Road. Tel: (020) 7416 5320; www.iwm.org.uk. Underground: Lambeth North. Open: 1000–1800 daily. ££ (children free). Free admission after 1630.

Some would say it is appropriate that a museum devoted to war should be located in a former madhouse – the **Bethlehem Royal Hospital**, from which the word 'bedlam' is derived. From the naval guns on the lawn and the military hardware (planes, submarines, a V2 rocket, a Polaris missile) in the entrance hall, you could be forgiven for thinking that this museum was all about tanks and guns. Nothing could be further from the truth – in fact, the museum is a stimulating and eloquent tribute to the suffering caused by **20th-century warfare**.

After seeing the exhibits in the main hall, most visitors head for the basement, where the **two World Wars** are explored through everything from Home Front posters to gas-masks and poignant letters from soldiers who never came home. Two popular attractions which just manage to avoid trivialising war are the **Trench Experience**, recreating the sights and sounds of the First World War and the **Blitz Experience**, set in a bombed-out London street during the Second World War. Devastating film footage from the Belsen concentration camp is to be shown as part of a new **Holocaust gallery**, housed in an extension to the museum from summer 2000. The museum is brought up to date with an exhibition on conflicts since 1945, including **Vietnam**, **the Falklands** and **the Gulf**. A sobering memorial pays tribute to the 100 million people killed in 20th-century wars and a quote from John F Kennedy speaks volumes about the horrors of war: 'Mankind must put an end to war, or war will put an end to mankind'.

London Aquarium, County Hall and the London Eye

Underground: Waterloo or Westminster.

To most Londoners, **County Hall** is best known as the former home of the **Greater London Council**, the body that, under its left-wing leader, **Ken Livingstone**, became a focus for opposition to the government of **Margaret Thatcher**. Thatcher took her revenge by abolishing the GLC in 1986. County Hall was sold off for development, so that when London finally regains its own government, the new mayor will be housed in a glass-covered building designed by Norman Foster, to be built on the South Bank beside HMS *Belfast* (*see page 127*) and due to be completed by 2001.

The basement of County Hall is now the **London Aquarium** (*tel: (020) 7967 8000; open: 1000–1800 daily; ££*), with an impressive array of sea creatures. Underwater tanks recreate the world's major marine ecosystems, with sharks, stingrays, stonefish and seahorses all on display. Also in County Hall, the **FA Premier League Hall of Fame** (*tel: 0870 848 8484; open: 1000–1800 daily; £££*) is devoted to Britain's footballing heroes.

Alongside County Hall, the **London Eye** is a dramatic and controversial addition to the skyline and has given Londoners an enjoyable new outlook on their city. The Eye, built for the millennium and due to stay for at least five years, is the world's largest observation wheel and the fourth tallest structure in London. The 30-minute ride inside one of 32 glass capsules gives spectacular views down over Big Ben – and has given Londoners the chance to relish looking down on the politicians in their palace across the water. *Tel: 0870 5000 600. Open: Apr–Oct, 0900–2200 daily; Nov–Mar, 1000–1800 daily. ££. Advance booking only.*

London Dungeon

34 Tooley Street. Underground: London Bridge. Tel: (020) 7403 0606. Open: Apr–Sept, 1000–1730 daily; Oct–Mar, 1000–1630 daily. £££.

This grisly tourist attraction, begun by a London housewife in 1975, has become one of the city's most visited sights. Teenagers love it here, but you should be wary of bringing young children or anyone of a nervous disposition. Situated in the dark tunnels beneath London Bridge, the Dungeon is a blood-curdling romp through the macabre sides of London's history, from plague pits and instruments of torture to the murders of Jack the Ripper. Wax tableaux, spooky effects and actors in period costume all add to the fun and the audience is encouraged to get involved. **Judgement Day**, an underground boat ride to a mock execution, is definitely not for the faint-hearted. The latest attraction is **Firestorm 1666**, a recreation of the Great Fire of London.

Old Operating Theatre, Museum and Herb Garret

9A St Thomas Street. Underground: London Bridge. Tel: (020) 7955 4791. Open: 1030–1700 daily. £.

If you prefer your blood and guts to be genuine rather than fake, ignore the London Dungeon in favour of this fascinating small museum. It may not quite have the same scream factor, but the horrors experienced here were real enough. The only surviving 19th-century operating theatre was discovered in 1956 when workmen drilled into the roof space of St Thomas's Church, used to carry out surgical operations for the neighbouring hospital. You can still see the bloodstains on the simple wooden operating table and almost hear the screams of the women patients who had to endure amputations without anaesthetic while medical students watched from the galleries.

Shakespeare's Globe

New Globe Walk. Box Office tel: (020) 7401 9919; www.shakespeares-globe.org.uk. Underground: Cannon Street or London Bridge. Riverboat to Bankside. Exhibition open: May–Sept, 0900–1230 daily; Oct–Apr, 1000–1700 daily. Theatre open: May–Sept. ££.

This unique reconstruction of an **Elizabethan playhouse** became the first thatched building in London since the Great Fire when it was completed in 1997. Inspired by the late **Sam Wanamaker**, the American theatre and film director, the 'Wooden O' is a faithful reproduction of the Globe Theatre which stood in a nearby street in Shakespeare's time. It was created from organic materials, such as reed, sedge, oak, lime and goat's hair, all held together without nails; beneath the floor of the arena is a layer of hazelnut shells, used in Shakespearean times to soak up the audience's urine. The stage, designed to resemble Italian marble, is actually made of wood. The authenticity extends to the productions, which take place in the open air between May and September, without amplification or stage lighting. There is still standing space, audience participation is encouraged and some of the productions have an all-male cast as in Shakespeare's day.

If you cannot make it to a play, try to go on one of the excellent **guided tours** that take place when the theatre is not in use. The tours include an exhibition on the history and traditions of the Bankside district, home to at least four theatres in Elizabethan times. Look out too for the wrought-iron gates facing on to the Thames, adorned with images from Shakespeare's plays. A second (indoor) theatre, the **Inigo Jones Theatre**, based on Jones's original design, will open in 2000 and will stage productions in winter.

South Bank Centre

Underground: Waterloo or Embankment. Riverboat to Festival Pier. For ticket information, *see page 176.*

London's biggest arts complex has developed on the South Bank as a result of the **1951 Festival of Britain**, a celebration of all things modern following the city's recovery from the Second World War. All that remains of the festival site is the **Royal Festival Hall**, a concert hall with excellent acoustics. Among other buildings to have been added since are the **National Film Theatre**, the **Hayward Gallery** (which stages major art exhibitions), the **Queen Elizabeth Hall** and the **National Theatre**. Although most Londoners now detest the brutalist 1960s architecture of the complex, they still come here to enjoy the views from the riverside terraces. There is also a second-hand book market, set up daily beside the river outside the National Film Theatre. This whole area is likely to undergo extensive renovation over the next few years. The **Museum of the Moving Image**, devoted to film and television, is closed until 2003; in the meantime, you can see a film at the new **BFI London Imax Cinema**, the largest cinema in Britain with a screen the height of five double-decker buses.

Tate Modern

25 Sumner Street. Tel: (020) 7401 7271; www.tate.org.uk. Underground: London Bridge or Southwark. Riverboat to Bankside. Open from 12 May 2000: Sun–Thur 1000–1800; Fri–Sat 1000–2200. £.

With the splitting up of the Tate Gallery (*see page 47*), one of the world's leading collections of **20th-century art** has finally found a suitable home in the former **Bankside Power Station**, designed by **Sir Giles Gilbert Scott** (the architect of the red telephone box), as a 'cathedral of power' facing St Paul's on the north bank.

By retaining the original façade and adding a glass roof and canopy, the architects, **Herzog and de Meuron**, have flooded the building with natural light and opened it up to both the river and the city. A new rooftop restaurant is entirely enclosed by glass, offering bird's-eye views across the river. The old Turbine Hall, 500ft long and 100ft high, has been converted into a stunning new exhibition space. The new building allows many works from the Tate's extensive collection of modern art to be shown for the first time. Major artists, such as **Picasso**, have a gallery to themselves, and other parts of the collection are arranged thematically, around topics such as war or the nude.

A sleek **millennium footbridge**, designed by Norman Foster and linking Tate Modern with St Paul's, is scheduled to open in 2000. As well as being a suitably modern addition to the London riverscape, the bridge provides a valuable pedestrian link between the north and south banks.

1 Bank End. Tel: (020) 7645 3700; www.vinopolis.co.uk. Underground: London Bridge; riverboat to Bankside. Open: 1000–1730 daily. £££.

Best described as an indoor theme park for grown-ups, Vinopolis is for everyone who loves wine. The main attraction is the Wine Odyssey, a multimedia journey through the history and geography of wine from its origins in ancient Georgia. Your ticket allows you to taste five wines chosen from around 200 on offer, including vintage port and champagne as well as fine wines from around the world. There is also a wine bar, a restaurant and shops selling wine and wine-related gifts.

Shopping

Bermondsey Antiques Market

Bermondsey Square. Underground: Borough. Open: Fri 0500–1400. Anyone interested in antiques should pay a visit to this sprawling market, the biggest in London. By the time the market opens to the public, dealers will already have snapped up many of the best goods, but it is still worth going just to browse through the huge range of antiques on offer.

Borough Market

On Saturdays, London's oldest surviving fruit and vegetable market (*Mon–Fri midnight–0700*) turns into a farmers' market, a great place to buy specialist foods from all over Britain, including organic meats, pork pies, cured bacon, farmhouse cheeses and speciality breads.

Gabriel's Wharf

This arty, villagey shopping mall (*shops open Tue–Sun 1100–1800*) is a great place for browsing. Among the craft shops here are **Vivienne Legg** (ceramics), **David Ashton** (bespoke jewellery) and **Ganesha** (fairly traded artefacts from India). A number of contemporary designers have their studios on the first and second floors of the nearby **Oxo Tower** (take the lift to the eighth-floor viewing gallery for one of the best riverside views in London).

Hay's Galleria

This converted Victorian wharf, beside London Bridge City pier, is now a stylish shopping complex, a pleasant place to break a riverside walk, with pavement cafés, restaurants and wine bars and occasional free jazz concerts.

Pubs

The **Founders Arms** is a modern riverside pub close to Tate Modern and Shakespeare's Globe, popular with City workers who enjoy the views from the picture windows and outdoor terrace. The food is a mixture of traditional English (fishcakes, sausages) and Mediterranean (lamb *tajine*). By contrast, the nearby **Anchor Inn**, beneath Southwark Bridge, was used by Shakespeare and Dr Johnson and retains much of its old-world appeal. Holding out against the gentrification of Borough Market, the **Market Porter** (*9 Stoney St*) is a genuine market pub, open from early morning with a good range of real ales. It also serves food at lunchtime. Not far from here, the **George Inn** (*77 Borough High St*) is London's last remaining galleried coaching inn, used by Shakespeare and Dickens and maintained by the National Trust. The pub serves Restoration ale, brewed locally, and hearty English fare such as fish and chips or bangers and mash. Plays are still performed in the courtyard in summer.

Restaurants

County Hall Restaurant

County Hall. Tel: (020) 7902 8000. ££. With views over the river, Big Ben and the London Eye, it's hard not to enjoy your meal at this smart restaurant inside the old County Hall. The menu is Modern European, with a mixture of the traditional and the innovative.

fish!

Cathedral Street. Tel: (020) 7836 3236. ££. This trendy fish restaurant is found in a Victorian glass pavilion on the edge of Borough Market. A menu lists which fresh fish is available; you can have it steamed or grilled, with a choice of five sauces. There is also a fresh fish shop next door.

Gourmet Pizza Company

Gabriel's Wharf. Tel: (020) 7928 3188. £. With riverside views, outdoor tables and avant-garde pizzas ranging from Cajun chicken to Camembert *calzone*, this funky pizzeria makes a good place to break a walk along the South Bank in summer.

Oxo Tower Brasserie

Oxo Tower. Tel: (020) 7803 3888. £££. Modern architecture, slate tables and huge picture windows overlooking the Thames make this restaurant on the top floor of the Oxo Tower a popular meeting place for the young, rich and beautiful. The food is Modern European with Pacific Rim influences.

Conranland

Style guru Terence Conran's restaurants at Butler's Wharf have become some of the hippest haunts in London. In theory, **Butler's Wharf Chop House** (*tel: (020) 7403 3403; ££*) serves British food, **Cantina del Ponte** (*tel: (020) 7403 5403; ££*) is Italian and **Le Pont de la Tour** (*tel: (020) 7403 8403; ££*) is French, but all tend to offer a similarly eclectic Modern European menu. Conran also owns the **Blueprint Café** (*tel: (020) 7378 7031; ££*), a more relaxed alternative above the Design Museum, and **The Apprentice** (*31 Shad Thames; tel: (020) 7234 0254; ££*), where students at his chefs' training school turn out creative dishes at reasonable prices.

Between June and August each year, the area around Gabriel's Wharf and Oxo Tower celebrates the Coin Street Festival, London's biggest free festival, with outdoor events including music and dance from around the world.

PROFILE

A riverside walk

There can be few more enjoyable experiences in London than a stroll along the South Bank of the Thames, admiring the great buildings of Westminster and the City across the water.

The Thames Path follows the river from source to sea, but for urban landscapes nothing can match the stretch between Lambeth and Tower Bridge. Many people find this walk particularly attractive at night, when the riverside pubs are full of lively chatter and the embankments are lit up like strings of pearls.

Besides the attractions listed elsewhere in this chapter, look out for the following:

Lambeth Palace is the official residence of the Archbishop of Canterbury, who, after the monarch, is head of the Church of England. The palace cannot be visited, but next door, in

Did you know?

Once the foulest river in Europe, the Thames is now one of the world's cleanest urban waterways, attracting more than 100 species of fish and birds. The muddy brown appearance of the water is a result of the tides, which travel inland as far as Twickenham.

the garden of the church of St Mary-at-Lambeth, is the intriguing **Museum of Garden History**. Among those buried in the attached cemetery are **John Tradescant**, who planted the first gardens here, and **Captain Bligh**, of *Mutiny on the Bounty* fame (*tel: (020) 7261 1891; open: Mar–Dec, Mon–Fri 1030–1600; Sun 1030–1700; £*).

The **Florence Nightingale Museum** is situated inside St Thomas's Hospital, where Florence Nightingale established the first modern school of nursing. Among the exhibits is the famous white lantern that earned her the nickname 'the lady of the lamp'. *Lambeth Palace Road. Tel: (020) 7620 0374. Open: Tue–Sun 1000–1700. £.*

The **Oxo Tower** is an art-deco warehouse converted into co-operative housing following a celebrated community campaign. A number of modern designers have their studios on the first floor. The complex includes the **Bernie Spain Gardens**, an offbeat shopping mall known as Gabriel's Wharf, and a wacky museum, the **Museum Of**, with changing exhibitions which are always designed to provoke.

Southwark Cathedral is one of London's oldest churches, begun in the 13th century as the church of St Mary Overie ('over the water') when Southwark was London's first suburb. The cathedral is hemmed in by bridges and railway viaducts, but ongoing restoration work will open it up to the river once again. Shakespeare's brother, Edmund, is buried here (*open: 0800–1800 daily; £*).

> “*Unreal City,*
> *Under the brown fog of a winter dawn,*
> *A crowd flowed over London Bridge, so many,*
> *I had not thought death had undone so many.*”

T S Eliot, *The Waste Land*, 1922

Greenwich and the Docks

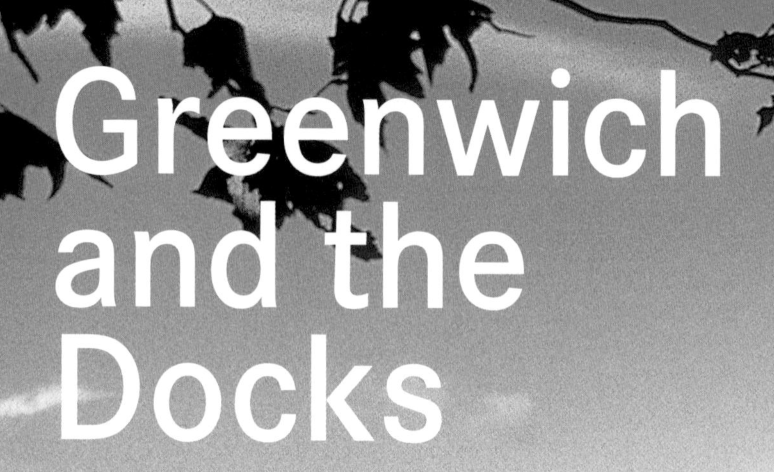

GREENWICH AND THE DOCKS

Maritime Greenwich is a World Heritage Site, home of the Maritime Museum and Royal Observatory, the Cutty Sark *and a lively street market, not to mention the Millennium Dome.*

Greenwich and the Docks

Getting there: it takes a mere 10 minutes to reach Greenwich from London Bridge station, with trains running every half hour or so. Combining ***tube*** *and* ***Docklands Light Railway*** *(DLR) takes longer (around 40 minutes from Central London), but ensures good views of the new architecture of the Docklands.*

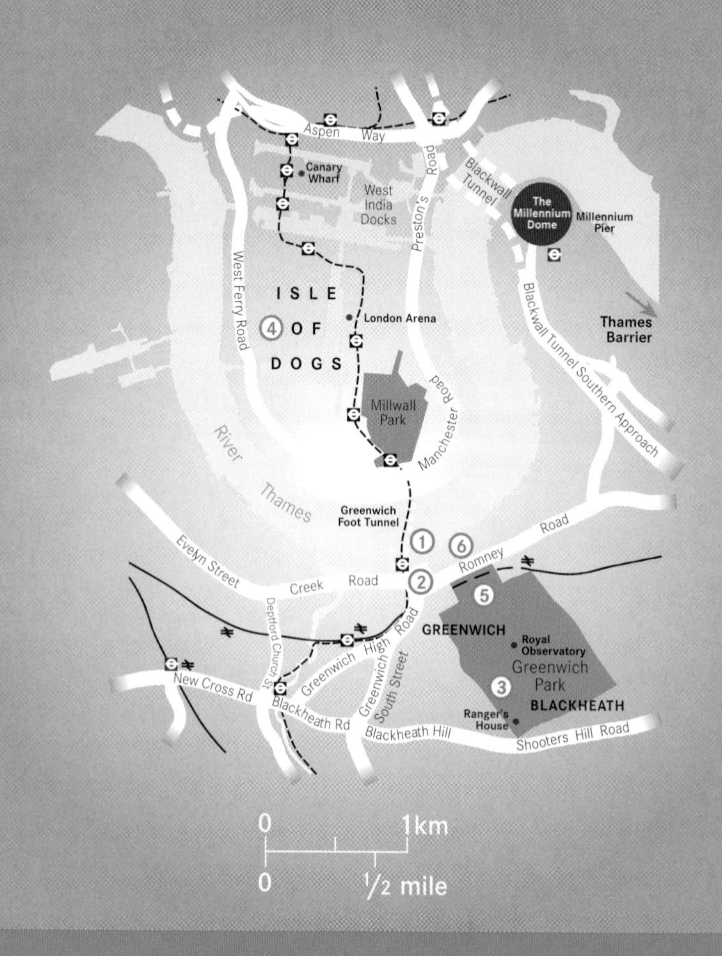

① Cutty Sark

Visit the last of the great tea clippers, launched in 1869, and compare its spacious quarters with the *Gypsy Moth IV*, moored alongside, in which Sir Francis Chichester made his solo voyage round the world in 1966–7. **Page 142**

② *Greenwich Markets*

Arts and Crafts every Thurs to Sun in the central covered market, antiques on Sat and Sun next to Greenwich Cinema, and the Village market, with crafts and organic food, on Sat and Sun in Stockwell Street. **Page 150**

③ *Greenwich Park*

This huge open space was created as a royal park in 1433, with sweeping views from its hills and terraces. Within the park are the **Royal Observatory** (*see page 149*), source of the world's time, and the aristocratic **Ranger's House** (*see page 143*), packed with artistic and architectural treasures. **Page 149**

④ *Isle of Dogs*

Accessible through the foot tunnel or by DLR, this new city in the east has some of London's most exciting modern architecture. **Pages 144–5**

⑤ *National Maritime Museum*

Everything you ever wanted to know about Britain's history as a seafaring nation, plus the Queen's House, England's first Renaissance building, designed by Inigo Jones as a royal villa in 1616–35. **Pages 146–7**

⑥ *The Old Royal Naval College*

Visit Sir Christopher Wren's architectural masterpiece, originally the Royal Hospital for Seamen, built between 1696 and 1751. **Page 148**

Tourist Information

A large and splendid new tourist information centre has opened in the Pepys House, in the grounds of the Old Royal Naval College, a short walk south of the *Cutty Sark* (*tel: (020) 8858 6376; open: daily 1000–1700*). Come here for maps and information on guided walks, events and accommodation in the area.

Tip

The cheapest way to enjoy Greenwich is to buy a combined ticket that includes entry to the Maritime Museum, the Royal Observatory and the Cutty Sark.

Cutty Sark

Cutty Sark Gardens. Tel: (020) 8858 4422. Open: Mon–Sat 1000–1800 (1700 in winter); Sun 1200–1800 (1700 in winter). ££.

Standing in a dry dock beside the Thames, the *Cutty Sark* is a splendid sight, and a solitary reminder that this stretch of the Thames would have once been crowded with river and sea-going craft, from clippers to humble barges. *Cutty Sark* was an anachronism from the start, because the year she was launched (1869) also saw the opening of the Suez Canal, which would open the Far East trade routes to steamers travelling via the Mediterranean, leading to the redundancy of clippers like the *Cutty Sark*, purpose-designed for the turbulent seas off Cape Horn.

Cutty Sark enjoyed a brief period as a tea clipper, breaking world records as she raced home from China bringing the first of the season's new crop of tea. In 1885, she switched to transporting wool from Australia, ending up as a training ship in the 1930s and finally as a beautifully restored relic of the great days of sail. Exhibits on the **Upper Deck** explain life on board and at sea; the **'Tween Deck** display covers the ship's history and restoration, and the **Hold** has a large collection of ship's figureheads.

Dwarfed by the *Cutty Sark*, ***Gypsy Moth IV*** stands alongside, the vessel in which **Sir Francis Chichester** followed the clipper passages of old to be the first to sail around the world solo. The 29,630-mile journey ended on 28 May 1967, after 226 days spent alone at sea.

Greenwich

Greenwich is a compact village of elegant Georgian houses and characterful shops, best visited at the weekend when the markets are in full swing. From Cutty Sark Gardens, King William Walk leads into the centre of the village, with the **Old Royal Naval College** (*see page 148*) on your left. Opposite, on the right, a narrow alley leads into the 19th-century **covered market** that hides behind the shop façades: permanent shops and craft stalls here sell everything from 1950s antiques to cut-price CDs and hand-crafted chocolates.

Emerging from the market on the opposite (western) side, you will see the tower of **St Alfege Church**, in Greenwich Church Street. This beautiful church, with its galleried interior and fine woodwork, was built by Nicholas Hawksmoor in 1718, on the site of the martyrdom of Alfege, Archbishop of Canterbury, killed by Vikings in 1012.

As you emerge from the church, **Stockwell Street**, focus of the bustling and friendly weekend market, is to your right. Heading up the street will take you to Croom's Hill, where you will find the **Greenwich Theatre**, noted for its excellent productions, and **Spread Eagle Yard**, an 18th-century coaching inn converted into antique shops, a pub and a restaurant.

Continue up **Croom's Hill** and you will pass a pleasing jumble of grand and humbler 17th and 18th-century buildings, many with blue plaques recording famous former residents. To see inside, visit the **Fan Museum** (*12 Croom's Hill; tel: (020) 8858 7879; www.fan-museum.org.uk; open: Tue–Sun 1100–1630, Sun 1200–1630; ££*) where you can learn all about the history and craft of fan-making whilst enjoying the superbly restored house or taking tea in the orangery.

Right at the top of Croom's Hill is the **Ranger's House**, a handsome building used to display a fine collection of Elizabethan and Jacobean paintings (*Chesterfield Walk; tel: (020) 8853 0035; www.english-heritage.org.uk; open: 1000–1800 daily in summer, shorter hours in winter; ££*).

The Isle of Dogs

Looking north from Greenwich, the cluster of massive towers that dominate the near horizon is a monument to the free-market capitalism of the 1980s, when London's former docks were swept away in favour of ambitious regeneration plans.

The main developers, Olympia & York, went into liquidation in the process and many investors lost large amounts of money, but today the sceptics have been proven wrong: the **Docklands** is a success, and London has a new architectural landmark in the form of Canary Wharf, the huge central tower that rises to 805ft, making it one of Europe's tallest buildings.

The opportunity to build on a greenfield site, without planning constraints, liberated architects to use their imaginations and to exploit modern constructional materials to create a stunning array of new office and housing developments. The result is an exciting and contemporary mix of New York, Hong Kong and Amsterdam, with 12-million-square-foot tower blocks interspersed with gardens, fountains and stretches of open water with bridges, boats and seagulls.

It is also worth exploring on foot, because traffic doesn't dominate. Centrepiece of the Isle of Dogs is **Canary Wharf**. Arrive here by **Jubilee Line** and you will step from the train into a cavernous and awe-inspiring modern station (opened in 1999) of cathedral-like proportions. The **DLR**, by contrast, leads straight into the bustling mall at the centre of Canary Wharf, with all the

wine bars, shops, hairdressers, florists and supermarkets needed to service the more than 250,000 people who live and work here.

Head west for **Cabot Square**, with its statues and fountains, and continue along West India Road and Westferry Circus (a traffic roundabout with a secluded and attractive park hidden in the centre of the island). This will bring you to the riverside walk, alongside **Canary Wharf Pier**, from where river boats carry commuters westwards to the City and Westminster.

Follow the riverwalk south from here if you want to enjoy the riverside architecture and sweeping views across to **Rotherhithe**, from where the Pilgrim Fathers set sail for America in the *Mayflower* in 1620 (the tall-masted barque you can see was built in 1952 as a training ship and now serves as a restaurant). Docklands Heritage noticeboards, located at intervals along the walk, explain the area's heritage, while cormorants sit preening on the mooring bollards and barges ply up and down the river. Lining the waterfront are buildings clearly inspired by ships and water, with names like the **Cascades** (the first lock south of the pier), penthouses projecting like crows' nests (the Shackleton Building and Pierpoint Building at **Millennium Harbour**), and sleek coning-tower curves (Ocean Wharf, next to the Sir John McDougall Gardens).

Just beyond the Gardens, you can cut inland along the path that passes between the Westferry Printing Works and the Docklands Sailing Club, passing beneath a pair of derrick cranes. Simply follow the path all the way alongside the Milwall Dock and you will eventually pass beneath another group of cranes to emerge beside the **London Arena** (for the Crossharbour and London Arena DLR station).

New for the Millennium

Opening in 2001, the ***Docklands Museum*** *will be housed in a historic warehouse on West India Quay and will bring together pictures, objects and personal memories to celebrate the history of London's once-thriving port (* see the London Tourist Board's website at www.londontown.com for further details *).*

The National Maritime Museum

The National Maritime Museum has organised its material under 16 well-chosen themes that draw together disparate material from the museum's vast reserves.

Once open to the sky, the museum's central courtyard has now been glassed over, and this covered courtyard at the heart of the complex contains the most contemporary displays – thought-provoking exhibits concerned with global warming, pollution, fishing and marine life and the future of our seas. The message is deliberately disturbing, and the same is true of many of the other galleries that lead off from this central courtyard: the displays ask as many questions as they answer.

In the gallery devoted to the theme of **Exploring beneath the sea**, video footage and a massive reconstruction of the rusting hull of the *Titanic* is accompanied by displays that ask us to ponder the question whether the quest for sunken treasure is driven by curiosity, the spirit of enquiry, the desire to explore the unknown, or the mercenary instincts of the treasure-hunter. The section on **Passengers** contrasts the spartan conditions of travellers in the functional third-class accommodation on board an ocean-going liner with the hotel-like luxury of the first-class deck. The sections dealing with war and with trade and empire also try to be even-handed in their perspective, giving equal weight to the point of view of the colonised as well as the colonists, of the foe as well as the friend.

Not everything in the museum comes accompanied by provocative commentary, however. The gorgeously carved and gilded royal barge of **Frederick, Prince of Wales**, from which he probably listened to the first performance of **Handel**'s *Water Music*, can be enjoyed for what it is – a frivolous but bravado piece of supreme craftsmanship. In the same vein, there are enjoyable displays on the influence of ships on architecture (think of Sydney Opera House, and the Ark in Hammersmith); on clothing and fashion as worn at sea and as worn on the High Street (remember bell-bottom trousers?); and on exotic cruises, with old P & O posters promising escape to romantic destinations.

Children are catered for in the **All Hands** gallery and the **Bridge**, both of which have interactive displays. Here you can try docking a catamaran in a busy harbour, piloting a paddle steamer, loading cargo into a ship without causing it to capsize or bombing your enemy into submission using an electronic cannon (no political correctness is allowed to intrude here!).

The **Queen's House**, linked to the Maritime Museum by a covered colonnade, is frequently used for special exhibitions, for which there is an additional entrance charge. The building is of great architectural interest, because it is England's first Renaissance building. Familiar as we now are with stone-built classical buildings, it is difficult to imagine the impact it had in the second decade of the 17th century when **Inigo Jones** built it as rural villa, or House of Delight, for the Stuart Court. Until then, London's buildings were of timber and thatch or of red brick and tile: imagine how exotic this building of crisp white stucco and stone would have looked by contrast. Inside is the glorious **Tulip Staircase**, a spiral stair completed at the height of the European tulip craze, with tulip flowers forming the main decorative motif of the wrought-iron balustrade.

Getting there: Greenwich Park. Tel: (020) 8312 6565; www.nmm.ac.uk.
Open: daily 1000–1700; closed 24–26 Dec. ££.

The Old Royal Naval College

Romney Road. Tel: (020) 8858 2256. Open: daily 1000–1700 (from 1230 on Sun); last admission 1600. ££ (visit the grounds for free).

Founded as the Greenwich Hospital for aged and infirm seamen in 1694, the Old Royal Naval College is a magnificent architectural ensemble, designed by **Sir Christopher Wren** and completed by Hawksmoor and Vanbrugh. The best place to appreciate Wren's grand design is from the river embankment, looking south up the central axis of the Hospital: here you can appreciate Wren's symmetrical design, with the two wings of the hospital framing the Queen's House on the hill above and the quirky Jacobean brick Observatory standing off centre to the right.

After serving as a Royal Naval Training College from 1873 to 1998, the buildings have recently been converted to form a campus for the **University of Greenwich**. Two buildings are open to the public: the baroque **Chapel** and the **Painted Hall**, so called because of its ceiling painting showing the monarchs William and Mary and allegorical figures symbolising the triumph of virtue over vice.

The Royal Observatory

Greenwich Park. Tel: (020) 8312 6575; www.rog.nmm.org.uk. Open: daily 1000–1700; last admission 1630. ££.

Star gazing

Alongside the Observatory is an excellent Planetarium** (shows every weekday afternoon, and on Sat afternoons Easter–end of Aug; tel: (020) 8312 6608 for details). **It costs extra to get in, but a fraction of the cost of a better-known establishment attached to Madame Tussaud's (and without the queues).

This curious building stands high on a terrace above the Thames with sweeping views across London. The fact that it was built out of old ship's timbers and recycled brick (from demolished buildings in the Tower of London) says much about the cheapskate nature of the original Royal Observatory enterprise, set up in 1675 to map the stars and, in so doing, to create better and more accurate navigational maps for commercial and naval shipping.

The hardships that successive Astronomers Royal endured while working at the Observatory form just one strand of a fascinating tale that is told very well by the displays here. Illustrated by original instruments and star maps, chronometers and state-of-the-art satellite images, this is the story of '**the Longitude Problem**', as it was known in the 17th century – the search for ways to measure time and position accurately at sea.

Central to this enterprise was the establishment of a fixed point from which time could be measured – hence the Greenwich (or Prime) Meridian, which has served us well as the world's standard for measuring time in the last two centuries, and could well become the standard for computers and the Internet in the 21st century. For most visitors this is irrelevant: they come for the novelty of standing astride the meridian line, with one foot in the eastern and one in the western hemispheres.

The Thames Barrier

1 Unity Way. Tel: (020) 8305 4188. Open: Mon–Fri 1000–1700 (last film shows at 1600); Sat–Sun 1030–1730 (last film shows at 1630). £.

This remarkable piece of engineering (completed in 1984) consists of ten movable gates, sheltered by sail-shaped hoods of steel, designed to protect London from flooding at times of exceptional tides, but also to let shipping pass unhindered. The excellent Visitors' Centre has a multimedia presentation explaining how and why it was built.

Shopping

The main attraction in Greenwich is the **covered market**, with quirky shops and specialist outlets: don't miss **Greenwich Printmakers**, selling original prints, posters and postcards by local artists; the exotic blooms and striking flower arrangements at **Rococo**; the designer jewellery at **Autumn & May**; the 1950s, 1960s and even 1970s kitsch at **Toot**; Asian artefacts at **Silk Route**; South American crafts at **Quetzal**; and the bargain-priced CDs at **Different Music**.

In Turnpin Lane, the alley leading out to Greenwich Church Street, look for **Ciao Bellina**, selling beautifully crafted chocolates and pâtisseries, and **Gypsy**, specialising in art-deco *objets d'art*.

Cheaper bargains, including antique and second-hand clothes, are found at the **Emporium**, on Greenwich Church Street, while almost next door is **Flying Duck Enterprises** where retro kitsch meets Hong Kong plastic in a shop full of corny novelties: anyone for a wind-up robot nun or a penis-shaped ketchup dispenser?

Market days are festive and atmospheric occasions in Greenwich. The Saturday market has organic food stalls, where you can buy fresh meat, fruit, veg, cheeses and bread to take home and cook, or you can sample ready cooked dishes in the Food Court. The antiques market runs on both Sat and Sun, though it is a bigger affair on Sun, with stalls selling books, comics, vinyl and CDs, antique clothing, furnishings, jewellery, china and collectables, plus all sorts of bric-à-brac.

Nightlife

Greenwich Theatre

10 Crooms Hill. Tel: (020) 8858 7755.

Closed in 1997 due to lack of funds, the newly revitalised Greenwich Theatre now hosts visiting productions, from new and classic drama, to the popular variety nights, providing an opportunity to enjoy sketches, songs, comedy routines, magic tricks and surprise acts.

Up the Creek

Creek Road. Tel: (020) 8858 4581.

Cabaret, jazz and comedy nights, plus bar and café serving Thai noodles.

Eating and drinking

Greenwich doesn't have any grand gourmet restaurants, but it does have a wide choice of good-value ethnic restaurants. In Greenwich Church Street, try **Tai Won Mein** (*No 49; tel: (020) 8858 1668; £; no credit cards*) for no-frills noodles at rock-bottom prices. On the opposite side of the road, the **Mogul Tandoori** (*No 10; tel: (020) 8858 6790; ££*) is a smart Indian with an informative menu and interesting variations on standard dishes (try salmon *tikka* or *lajawab jhingra* – king prawn in coconut milk and spices). Almost alongside are **Beachcomber** (*No 34; tel: (020) 8858 5124; ££*), specialising in fish and seafood, and **Ciao Bellina** (*No 18; tel: (020) 8305 1720; ££*), where you can feast on a huge bowl of mussels or choose from the extensive pizza and pasta menu.

In Creek Road, the smart **Kum Lang** is so popular that you would be wise to book (*Nos 326–8 Creek Road; tel: (020) 8293 4011; lunch Fri–Sun, dinner daily; ££*); locals flock for authentic Thai cuisine, including a good range of vegetarian food.

Nelson Road has the Mexican **Café Sol** (*No 13; tel: (020) 8853 4385; ££*), where the menu ranges from chargrilled swordfish to Mexican sausage and blazing hot chilli sauce. Opposite is another good-value Japanese eatery called **Noodle Time** (*No 10; tel (020) 8858 9884; £*) where it costs almost nothing to fill up on tasty rice or noodle dishes. More expensive, but still good value, is **La Cucina di Soteri** (*No 1; tel (020) 8858 8424; ££*), a modern Italian serving large pizzas and bowls of sustaining pasta.

Slightly out of the centre is the up-market **Spread Eagle**, a French restaurant opposite the Greenwich Theatre (*2 Stockwell Street; tel: (020) 8853 2333; £££*) and the historic **Trafalgar Tavern**, with its bow windows looking out over the Thames and a menu of traditional fish dishes, from smoked eel to Trafalgar whitebait (*Park Row; tel: (020) 8858 2437; ££*).

The Isle of Dogs has **Ken Hom**'s pan-oriental **Yellow River** (*Canary Wharf, North Colonnade; tel: (020) 7715 9515; closed Sun*) with a downstairs café (*££*) and an upstairs restaurant (*£££*), where Malaysian *laksa*, Sichuan duck, Singapore curry noodles, Thai red beef curry and Vietnamese crispy chilli fish all co-exist happily on the same menu. Alongside the London Arena, the **Lotus Floating Restaurant** (*38 Limeharbour, Inner Milwall Dock; tel: (020) 7515 6445; ££*) is a must for lovers of authentic Cantonese food, serving dishes rarely found outside Hong Kong, including delicious prawns, beef and rice baked in lotus leaves.

The Millennium Dome

If you are a teenager (in age or in spirit) you will love the Dome: it is entertaining and memorable, even if you do have to put up with a bit of a queue.

The highlight of the Dome has to be the spectacular **Millennium Show**, which is performed five times a day, a 45-minute carnival and high-flying acrobatic display created by pop impresarios **Peter Gabriel** and **Mark Fisher** (clue: the plot centres around a love affair between a dreamy boy and an all-action girl – it's a bit like Romeo and Juliet except that the figures symbolise the relationship between nature and technology).

On the loudness scale, it is beaten by the giant heart pumping blood in the **Body Zone**, which has so far proved to be the most popular of the 14 themed zones in the Dome. If queues and noise are not your thing, head for the **Faith Zone** where you can sit in quiet contemplation of matters transcendental, or crash out in the **Rest Zone**, with its ambient music and soft, sleep-inducing floor.

Do you know someone with excess energy to burn? Steer then towards the mayhem of the **Play Zone**, full of interactive games of the old-fashioned kind (where you have to use human force and skill) and of the digital kind – computer games of the future.

After physical exertion, what about some mental stimulation? **Home Planet** takes you on a space flight to look back down on the fragile blue Earth and then contrasts life in the UK with those of people living in China, Israel and America. The global village message is more overt in **Living Island**, where environmental issues are tackled, and in **Money**, where the future of virtual cash is explored. Stimulated by this, check out the **Learning Zone**, where the bad old past of smelly school corridors is contrasted with the fragrant

Learning Orchard of the digital future – yes, it's all a bit idealistic, naive and simplistic, but most visitors to the Dome seem happy to suspend their sense of reality, at least for the day.

Getting there: there is a 2-mile **No Car Zone** around the Dome, so you must come by **public transport**. The cheapest and fastest option is to take the Jubilee line to North Greenwich station (the tube exit is right next to the Dome). Alternatively, there are riverboat services from Waterloo (*tel: (020) 7237 5134 for details or pick up a Thames river services leaflet from underground stations*).

Tickets: it is best to book these in advance rather than queue at the Dome. They can be purchased from National Lottery retailers, from the Dome website (*www.dome2000.co.uk*) or by phoning the Dome Ticket Line on 0870 606 2000.

Opening times: daily 1000–1800, with late night opening some evenings to 2300 (ticket sellers have details).

Best deal: go as a 'family', if you can: the 'Family Five' ticket (one adult and four children or two adults and three children) represents the cheapest way to see the Dome.

Catering: there's plenty of choice, with many High Street chains represented here, from Yo! Sushi and the New Covent Garden Soup Company to the inevitable McDonald's.

Further afield

FURTHER AFIELD

If you're gasping for a change of scenery – some green fields in place of concrete and tarmac – head out to Tudor Hampton Court, or scale the heights of Hampstead and Highgate for great views and a breath of fresh air.

Chiswick House

Burlington Lane, Chiswick. Tel: (020) 8995 0508; www.english-heritage.org.uk. Open: Apr–Oct daily 1000–1700; rest of year Wed–Sun 1000–1600; closed 24–26 and 1–18 Jan. £.

Chiswick House is a little piece of Italy set down in a west London suburb, a place of escape and rural retreat that could be on the outskirts of Rome or Venice but for the very English trees that surround it and the often dull English weather. The delightful villa was built in 1725–9 by **Lord Burlington** as a temple to the Arts, but the many paintings of voluptuous nudes masquerading as classical goddesses shows that this patron of the arts has a fine appreciation of earthly as well as intellectual delights. Lord Burlington designed the villa himself as a tribute to his two great architectural heroes: **Andrea Palladio**, whose Villa Capra (also known as the Villa Rotonda), near Vicenza, was the inspiration for Chiswick House and **Inigo Jones**, the great English pioneer of classical architecture. Statues of both men (by Rysbrack) stand either side of the fine double staircase leading up to the lavishly decorated public rooms, beautifully restored to their original splendour by English Heritage. From the rooms there are views of the beautiful gardens that surround the villa, dotted with statues and temples in imitation of the landscape of the Roman Campagna.

Tip

*A visit to Chiswick House and Hogarth's House can be combined with a trip to nearby Kew Gardens (*see page 162*). Alternatively, you can take the underpass from Hogarth's House and walk down Church Lane to the River Thames. Here you can walk eastwards for just over a mile along Chiswick Mall past some of London's best-preserved 18th-century houses, with colourful gardens and some excellent riverside pubs. The walk takes you to Hammersmith where you can catch a tube back to central London.*

Within walking distance of Chiswick House and just to the north, stands **Hogarth's House** (*Hogarth Lane; tel: (020) 8994 6757; open: winter 1300–1600, summer 1300–1700, closed Mon and Jan; £*), the summer retreat of the great 18th-century satirical painter. The 'little country box by the Thames', as Hogarth described it, is hung with a comprehensive collection of his satirical engravings – over 200 in total – and with copies of his famous work, *The Rake's Progress* (the originals are in the Sir John Soane Museum – *see page 101*).

Dulwich Picture Gallery

College Road, Dulwich. Tel: (020) 8693 5254. Open: 1000–1700; closed Mon. £.

Frequently billed as London's least-visited museum, the newly refurbished Dulwich Picture Gallery is home to a remarkable collection of 300 Old Masters, including works by **Rembrandt** (his portrait of *Jacob III van Gheyn*), **Van Dyck** (*Madonna and Child*) and **Poussin** (*The Return of the Holy Family from Egypt*). The remarkable collection was put together by art dealer **Noel Desenfans** in 1790, acting for the king of Poland who planned to open a national gallery in Warsaw. When the king was deposed, Desenfans offered the collection to the British Government, but they said no thanks and the collection was eventually bequeathed to Dulwich College in 1811, which explains why this quiet and leafy London suburb has an art collection as good as any in the world.

From the gallery, you can walk east across Dulwich Common to visit the **Horniman Museum** (*London Road, Forest Hill; tel: (020) 8699 2339; open: Mon–Sat 1030–1730, Sun 1400–1730*). Housed in a fine art-nouveau building, this quirky museum has an outstanding collection of **African art** and excellent **natural history** section devoted to ecology and environmental understanding.

Hampton Court Palace

Hampton. Tel: (020) 8781 9500; www.hrp.org.uk. Open: Mon 1015–1800 (1630 mid-Oct–mid-Mar); Tue–Sun 0930–1800 (1630 mid-Oct–mid-Mar); closed 24–26 Dec and 1 Jan. £££.

Hampton Court Palace is easily reached by train (Waterloo to Hampton Court; journey time 32 minutes) but if you have the time, the only way to get to the Palace is to come by river, just as Henry VIII did when the palace was splendid and new. River launches run to Hampton Court from Westminster, via Kew and Richmond, at 1015, 1030, 1115, 1200 and 1400 daily in summer (but check with the operator on *(020) 7930 2062*, because times can vary according to the tides).

The Palace itself is vast: built by **Cardinal Wolsey**, it was intended to be the most splendid palace in the land. To aspire to outdo any monarch in this respect was, of course, an act of hubristic folly. **Henry VIII** (who, in 1536, would seize the assets of 361 wealthy English monasteries for his own use) suggested to Wolsey that he might like to make a present of Hampton Court to his monarch. How could Wolsey resist? He handed the palace to Henry in 1525 and the king (showing where his priorities lay) immediately added the impressive Tudor Kitchens and the Great Hall, capable of feeding the 1,000-strong royal retinue.

The **Tudor Kitchens** form the highlight of one of the six different routes on offer at Hampton Court, each route revealing a different aspect of royal life at the palace. The **Great Hall**, with its spectacular hammerbeam roof, and the **Chapel Royal** form the highlights of the route devoted to **Henry VIII's State Apartments**, popular because it includes the **Haunted Gallery**, where the ghost of Catherine Howard, fifth wife of Henry VIII (beheaded for adultery), is said to utter piercing screams as she protests her innocence. The **Wolsey Rooms** display important Renaissance paintings and give a sense of the appearance of the earliest palace, whereas the **Queen's State Apartments**, the **Georgian Rooms** and the **King's Apartments** (beautifully restored after the 1986 fire) are all concerned with the later additions, built around Sir Christopher Wren's elegant **Fountain Court**.

An energetic visitor could take in all six routes in one visit, but don't forget to allow some time to visit the 60 splendid acres of Tudor, baroque and Victorian gardens that surround the palace. From the patterned formality of the **Dutch Garden** to the burgeoning borders of the **Tiltyard Gardens** and the tree-filled, deer-grazed landscape of **Home Park**, the whole sweep of English gardening history is exemplified here. Queen Anne's contribution was the famous **Maze**, planted in 1714, and still pulling in people with a taste for puzzles. Don't worry if you get totally lost: someone does come round and rescue stray souls at the end of the day …

"There it lay in the early sunshine of spring. It looked like a town rather than a house … courts and buildings, grey, red, plum colour … some oblong, some square; in this was a fountain, in that a statue … while smoke from innumerable chimneys curled perpetually into the air … (a) vast, yet ordered building, which could house a thousand men."

Virginia Woolf, *Orlando*, 1928

Hampstead and Highgate

Today you would have to pay a large sum of money to buy a house here, but 'Ham and High' was cheap enough in the past to attract artists and intellectuals, including a large colony of Middle European and Russian émigrés.

Pre-eminent among the latter was **Karl Marx**, whose grave in **Highgate East Cemetery** is an object of pilgrimage for visitors from around the globe (*Swain's Lane; tel: (020) 8340 1834; open: East Cemetery core hours are 1100–1600 daily, with longer hours in summer; West Cemetery by guided tour daily from noon in summer, but Sat and Sun only in winter; £*). Both cemeteries are worth visiting for their wealth of funerary architecture, the romantic atmosphere and the graves of such eminent Victorians as Mary Anne Evans (aka the author **George Eliot**), **Christina Rossetti** and **Michael Faraday**.

Sigmund Freud escaped to London from Nazi persecution in Vienna in 1938. His house (with its famous couch and a reconstruction of his Viennese study) is now the **Freud Museum** (*20 Maresfield Gardens, Hampstead; tel: (020) 7435 2002; open: Wed–Sun 1200–1700; £*).

Goldfinger

Ian Fleming, author of the James Bond stories, so detested the functional style of the tower blocks and houses designed by Erno Goldfinger that he named one of his worst villains after him.

Hungarian émigré **Erno Goldfinger** also arrived in the 1930s and introduced the Modernist style of architecture to Hampstead. His house at **2 Willow Grove** (*tel: (020) 7435 6166; open: 1 Apr–30 Oct, Thur, Fri and Sat by guided tour every 45 mins; first tour starts 12.15, last starts 1600; £*)

is now owned by the National Trust. Highlights include the introductory film explaining the origins and influence of the Modernist style, the works of art by the likes of **Max Ernst** and **Henry Moore** and the furnishings, which Goldfinger himself designed to go with the house.

More conventionally pretty houses abound in the area. In Hampstead you can visit **Keats House** where the poet lived from 1818 to 1820 (*Wentworth Place, Keats Grove, Hampstead; tel: (020) 7435 2062; open: core hours are 1000–1300 and 1400–1700, with afternoon-only opening on Sun and in winter; £*), or you can wander down pretty **Church Row** and **Holly Walk** to admire the creeper-clad houses, with their pretty front gardens and ornate railings. **Fenton House**, built in 1693 in the Dutch style fashionable in the reign of William and Mary, has delightful gardens and an important collection of musical instruments (*Hampstead Grove; tel: (020) 7435 3471; open: Apr–Oct, Wed–Sun 1400–1700; £*).

To the north lies the vast expanse of **Hampstead Heath**, a good place for a walk (though the Heath is best avoided at night). **Parliament Hill**, the highest point, rises to 319ft and enjoys fine views over the city. To the north east are several ponds used for bathing in summer and further north still is the grassy amphitheatre and lake that is used for open-air concerts on Saturday nights in summer (*details from English Heritage; tel: (020) 7973 3434*).

Kenwood House sits on the northern edge of the Heath (*Hampstead Lane; tel: (020) 8348 1286; www.english-heritage.org.uk; open daily 1000–1600, with later opening in summer; £*). This stately Adam-designed house contains over 1,000 pictures, including such outstanding works of art as **Rembrandt**'s brooding *Portrait of the Artist* and **Vermeer**'s *The Guitar Player.*

Kew Gardens

Glorious Kew is worth a day of anyone's time. The Royal Botanical Gardens have been aptly described as a great museum on a par with those in central London, but the exhibits here are alive and flourishing and they come in every strange, evocative and stirring shape and colour that nature is capable of devising. In addition, the historic buildings, from the Palm House to the Pagoda, are wonders in their own right.

The best way to get to Kew is by **riverboat.** Services from Westminster Pier operate from April to the end of September: phone the boat operator on *(020) 7930 2062* for details, or pick up *Thames River Services* leaflets from London Transport information centres.

Your priorities on arrival will depend on the time of year. In early spring (from February) the green grass is studded with crocuses, planted in drifts of jewel-like colour. Daffodils and tulips follow in unbroken succession, to be followed by frothy masses of flowering cherry and then by the many and varied hues of azaleas and rhododendrons.

Even in the depths of winter, when all is grey outside, the conservatories and glasshouses provide an escape to a warmer and more exotic world. The most recently completed is the modern **Princess of Wales Conservatory**, whose low tent-like glass roofs shelter a variety of microclimates. Cactuses and stone-like lithops thrive in the bone-dry desert area, while another part of the conservatory is packed with the exotic blooms of the world's biggest collection of orchids.

Among the older glasshouses, the **Palm House** and the **Temperate House**, both designed by Decimus Burton in the 1840s and 1850s, seem to reflect the organic forms of the palms and greenhouse plants that they contain. In fact, the buildings, of wrought-iron and glass, are giant inverted boats, borrowing techniques from the shipyard rather than the natural world. Elevated galleries and walkways within the

greenhouses enable you to climb to the treetops and experience the rainforest from the canopy. Among the exotic and multi-coloured plants, the stars are the giant Amazonian lilies, with leaves up to 2 metres across.

By the time these buildings were put up, Kew was already at the forefront of botanical research, filled with newly discovered plants sent back by plant hunters as famous as Captain Cook and Sir Joseph Banks. Before this, Kew was more a pleasure park than a serious academic venture and the buildings that survive from the 18th century reflect the taste for novelty. The delightful 10-storey **pagoda**, for example, was built in 1762 and offers great views over the treetops. **Queen Charlotte's Cottage**, built in the 1770s, was where **King George III**'s queen played at being a simple shepherdess: now it is charmingly planted with British native wildflowers, including swathes of bluebells in May.

Getting there: Kew, Richmond, Surrey. Tel: (020) 8940 1171.
Open: daily 0930 to dusk. ££.

Lifestyles

Shopping, eating, children and nightlife in London

Shopping

Shopping is rapidly becoming the *preferred leisure activity of the majority of the population, and London caters exceedingly well for all kinds of addicts: bargain hunters, window browsers, book lovers, fashion victims, novelty seekers* et al.

For the most concentrated shopping experiences, head for **Oxford Street**, where all the big High Street names have their flagship stores, from Marks & Spencer at the Marble Arch end of Oxford Street to Virgin at the other, with HMV, H&M, Top Shop, Borders, Next, Gap, Muji and many more in between.

Regent Street fancies itself as being a little more up-market, with the likes of Burberry, Aquascutum, Jaeger and Country Casuals, aimed at American and Japanese shoppers, but also the joys of Dickins & Jones (excellent fashions), Liberty (from crafts to clothes) and Hamley's (five floors packed with toys and excited children). At the **Piccadilly Circus** end of the street, Tower Records is the place where you are almost certain to find any record or video, and Waterstones (on the south side of Piccadilly) is your best bet for books.

Alternatives

Covent Garden still retains its 'alternative' edge with quirky shops devoted to Oriental artefacts, cheese, wholefoods or buttons and beads, though there are many mainstream shops as well in the new arcade that wraps round the opera house side of the piazza. In the **piazza**, buskers entertain, and stallholders sell all sorts of crafts – from jewellery and hair ornaments to wind chimes and dream catchers – at prices most people can afford. On the other hand, if your tastes run to designer fashion, with price no object, Covent Garden's side streets (notably **Floral Street**) have some

tempting windows displaying the creations of such fashion leaders as **Paul Smith** and **agnès b**.

Back to basics, one of the most enjoyable places to shop in London at the moment is **Spitalfields Market** (*opposite Liverpool Street Station*), a friendly place to browse for clothes, crafts, records and organic food, which hasn't yet become as commercialised or as crowded as the larger **Camden Lock Market** (*see page 82*).

Can't afford it, but fun to look

London is full of seriously rich people. Where their money comes from it is perhaps best not to ask. Most citizens who haven't got a lot of spare cash are still allowed to dream of what they would do if they won the National Lottery. For inspiring ideas, stroll along **South Molton Street** or **New Bond Street** and admire the window displays of the world's leading *couturièrs*.

Towards the southern end of New Bond Street, chic clothing boutiques give way to world-renowned art galleries where handsome pictures change hands for prices that will not leave much change from a million. Thank goodness for the **Fine Art Society** (*146 New Bond Street*), which has excellent exhibitions and a good range of paintings, drawing and sculpture at prices that even the ordinary art lover can just about begin to afford.

Trading hours

London shops open lateish (1000 is normal) but stay open longer than most. As a general rule, Knightsbridge and Chelsea has Wednesday as its late-opening night, and West End shops are open to 1930 or 2000 on Thursday night, though many are open as late as this every day – except for Sunday, where current trading laws dictate a maximum of six hours, so everything will be shut by 1800.

Eating out

Restaurateurs can still be heard to moan from time to time that Londoners are Philistines and are not prepared to spend money on eating out. By contrast with our gourmet American or Continental cousins, we were branded a nation of killjoys who would rather sit at home with a video eating supermarket meals than go out and spend money on good food and wine.

This, of course, is nonsense: Londoners are no different to Parisians, New Yorkers or Romans – we love eating out, we just don't like being ripped off. Those restaurateurs that have got the message and offer interesting menus at realistic and competitive prices now attract diners in droves. Compared with two decades ago when people rarely ate out, Londoners now eat out on average three times a week!

Eating ethnic

Londoners tend to apply a simple test to restaurant prices: 'what would it cost me to cook this same dish at home'. If the restaurant price is not excessively marked up, and the cooking is competent, people will flock. Ethnic restaurants have done best from this golden rule because they serve a range of exotic food at prices that could hardly be matched by the home cook, with the added appeal of novelty value: everyone knows how to grill a competent steak, but few Londoners have the skills, ingredients and equipment to cook up a Thai, Goanese, Shanghainese or Japanese dish.

Food critics and guides remain eternally snobbish about 'ethnic' restaurants, despite the fact that many of the best chefs respect Asian cooking as one of the world's great cuisine styles, on a par with French/ Continental. **Michelin**, the food guide of Francophile snobs, has

reluctantly started to list ethnic restaurants in its UK edition, but has ghettoised them in a separate category, as if to say, 'these are not true restaurants'.

Luckily, Londoners and visitors with a taste for the exotic know differently and can enjoy good-value food from just about every nation under the sun. Increasingly, too, ethnic restaurants are going back to authentic cuisine, rather than cooking up a westernised version of standard dishes. Ethnic restaurants are everywhere, and the best guide to the complete range is the ***Time Out Eating and Drinking Guide***, sold in numerous shops and newsagents. Good places tend to concentrate in certain areas, so if you just want to browse, head for **Chinatown** (Gerrard Street and Wardour Street in Soho) for Peking-style, Cantonese and *dim sum* dishes, **Brick Lane**, in Spitalfields, for Bangladeshi food, and **Drummond Street** (behind Euston station) for an exciting range of southern Indian food (including vegetarian restaurants) at astonishingly low prices.

Is there an English cuisine?

English cooking is a strange beast, which most people know when they encounter it but few can define. At one extreme it is defined by the food served in London's ubiquitous sandwich bars and cafés, known affectionately as '**greasy spoons**' because of their alleged lack of cleanliness and the prevailing atmosphere of fatty fug. Mostly run by anglicised Italians, they serve the quintessentially English dishes of 'all day breakfast', beans (or cheese) on toast or bacon butties. One step up is the **pub**, where the signature dishes are shepherd's pie, steak and kidney and roast beef. All are cheap, nourishing and tasty, if a little lacking in subtlety.

Top of the tree are the so-called **new British restaurants**, which seem either to serve up-market versions of fish and chip shop favourites, or offal. Visit the up-and-coming **Clerkenwell** area if you want to sample this kind of food: St John Street and Cowcross Street have a good selection of well-regarded restaurants located in converted warehouses and industrial buildings.

The old rules

There is another kind of English cooking that is best represented by the **top hotel dining rooms** (the Connaught, the Ritz) or by institutions such as Simpson's on the Strand or Rules (*35 Maiden Lane*). Here the style of cooking is historical, based on the sort of food consumed by the **Edwardian gentry**: beef, carved with great ceremony from a trolley, game in various forms, salmon (wild – not farmed) and steamed puddings. Steak houses masquerade as a popular and inexpensive alternative, but there is no substitute for the real thing, if you can afford it.

Gourmet temples

Dedicated foodies determined to sample the food of a renowned chef will be able to do so with persistence. The best restaurants have waiting lists a month long, and any restaurant that has recently been reviewed favourably in the national press will be fully booked up for months after the review appears. However, this tends to be true only for evening meals: **lunchtime** is a different matter, and many top restaurants serve an excellent fixed-price lunchtime menu that will enable you to worship at the feet of your chosen hero without having to take out a large bank loan.

Rituals

The renaissance of good food in London has its downsides. One is that it is now almost **_de rigueur_ to book**. If you plan to eat out in central London on Friday or Saturday night, you probably will not get a table unless you do. Even inexpensive chain restaurants have **queues**.

Another problem is the shortage of competent waiting **staff**. Think yourself lucky if your waiter/waitress is merely charmingly incompetent. Many are downright intrusive, and take great pleasure in humiliating their clients with subtle and not so subtle putdowns. Don't think that complaining will help: waiters do not belong to the 'customer is always right' school of management; instead, they have learned the American business-school concept that there are always at least two perspectives on any issue and that the waiter's perspective is as valid as yours. No matter how incompetent and intrusive, your waiter will still expect a **10 per cent tip** (as a minimum).

Supermarket sushi

Never forget that there is an alternative. Along with the boom in restaurants, so has there been an increase in the quality and range of food available from even the most unlikely sources. Would you eat in a **bookshop**? Many people do, now that some of London's big bookstores have excellent cafés selling salads, soups and sandwiches, or full meals. Fancy a **department store**? From baked spuds and pizza at BHS (British Home Stores) to sushi and pickled seaweed at Harvey Nichols, there's a great range of food on offer in London's in-store cafés. As for takeaway food, look out for sushi and gourmet sandwiches at Marks and Spencer – miles better value than anything sold in the more conventional sandwich shops.

London with children

What you do in London with children depends on your attitude (and theirs) to queuing. They will try and propel you in the direction of **Madame Tussaud's** (*see page 62*), but you are unlikely to get in without standing in a long line for a couple of hours – not too bad if the sun is shining and you have plenty of diversionary games to play, but no fun at all in howling wind and chilling rain. Some people claim that Westminster Abbey's **Undercroft Museum** (*tel: (020) 7233 0019; open: 1030–1600; £*) makes an acceptable alternative, but only if your children are likely to be interested in wax funerary effigies of James I, Charles II or Horatio, Viscount Nelson. These astonishing figures, dressed in their own clothes and made to be carried in state funerals, are fascinating, but that may not impress children bent on seeing Madonna or the Spice Girls.

Good and not-so-good museums

Pretty well guaranteed to appeal to any child are the classics of **London Zoo** (*see page 60*), the **Natural History Museum** (*see page 26*) and the **Science Museum** (*see page 28*). Also good because of their interactive exhibits or hands-on approach are the **Imperial War Museum** (especially the Blitz Experience – *see page 128*) and the **London Transport Museum** (*see page 103*). Some museums that seem aimed at children are actually far from being child-friendly: few children enjoy the **Bethnal Green Museum of Childhood** because the exhibits are locked in cases and cannot be touched, and the same applies to the very serious approach taken by **Pollock's Toy Museum** and the **Theatre Museum**

School holiday events

On the other hand, even these museums come into their own when it comes to special events for children, and this is an area in which all museums seem to excel, especially at weekend and during school holidays, so it is well worth buying a magazine, such as *Kids Out*, or visiting the museum websites to find out what is going on. Among the best museums for children's activities, including role playing, art and craft and storytelling, are the **Victoria and Albert Museum** (*see page 30*), the **Museum of London** (*see page 113*) and the **British Museum** (which organises very popular sleepovers where children get to spend the whole night in the spooky Egyptian Gallery – *see page 80*).

Shop 'til you drop

Children love shopping just as much as the grown ups – the only problem is that the girls in your family will want to visit different shops from the boys. The best compromise is to head for an area like **Covent Garden** that has enough variety to please everyone. Alternatively, head for **Oxford Circus** and go your separate ways for an hour: the computer games and toys of Hamley's or Virgin will act as a magnet to the boys, whereas the girls have the choice of Miss Selfridge, Top Shop, H&M or New Look.

Eating out

Smollensky's Balloon, the American brasserie, offers brunch at the weekends complete with computer games, clowns and colourful non-alcoholic cocktails (*105 Strand; tel: (020) 7497 2101; open: 1200–1500 Sat and Sun; ££*). In a similar vein, **TGI Fridays** (*6 Bedford Street; tel: (020) 7379 0585; ££*) has a magician, face-painting and balloons from noon to 1700 on Sat and Sun. The **Rainforest Café** (*20 Shaftesbury Avenue; tel: (020) 7434 3111; ££*) is open every day and is reminiscent of Disney, with its thunder, lightening, waterfalls and animated crocodiles, plus American-style food.

After Dark

Going out after dark is half the point of living in London: few other cities have such a rich choice of nightlife activities, from pub theatre, drag acts and comedy clubs to world-class opera, dance and classical music.

Booking ahead

For the most popular and prestigious events – stadium-rock concerts and sell-out musicals – you simply will not get in unless you book in advance. The hassle-free way to do this is to use one of the large ticket agencies: they frequently have tickets for events that are otherwise sold out. Yes, you pay a hefty price for the service, but this may be the only chance you get to see your favourite band or show. Ticket agencies are found all along Charing Cross Road and Shaftesbury Avenue, or you can phone:

- **First Call** (*tel: (020) 7420 0000; www.firstcalltickets.com*)
- **Ticketmaster** (*tel: (020) 7413 1442; www.ticketmaster.co.uk*)
- **Ticket Select** (*tel: (020) 7494 5394; www.ticketselect.co.uk*).

Significant group discounts are available if you can put together a group of 10 or more friends. An agency specialising in group bookings is **LTB** (*tel: (020) 7494 0741; www.londontheatrebookings.com*).

Last-minute decisions

On the other hand, if you are not fussy about what you want to see, there are some excellent bargains to be had by turning up at the last minute. Unsold tickets are often sold off cheaply within an hour or so of the start of the performance, and midweek ticket sales, especially in winter, are rarely as brisk as Friday and Saturday night sales in summer. Last-minute tickets for classical music concerts at the Barbican or Festival Hall (*see below*) can be very good value. Theatre lovers can use the **Half-price ticket booth**, located in the clock tower building on Leicester Square (*open: Tue–Sun 1200–1830*), for sales of tickets for that day's performances – personal callers and cash only for tickets sold at half price, plus a small service charge.

The major venues

London is home to some of Britain's best artists in their respective fields, and almost any performance at the following venues is bound to be a winner.

Barbican Centre (*Silk Street; tel: (020) 7638 4141, www.barbican.org.uk*). The Barbican Centre is home to the **London Symphony Orchestra**, but also serves as a venue for leading orchestras and soloists, with excellent family concerts and themed months. You can also enjoy music for free in

the foyer before performances. The theatre here is the London home of the Royal Shakespeare Company, which divides its time between the Barbican and Stratford, bringing new and classical works to the stage, as well as the works of the Bard. The Centre's cinema also shows classics from the film repertoire.

London Coliseum (*St Martin's Lane; tel: (020) 7632 8300*). Ballet performances during Christmas and summer give way to the **English National Opera**'s outstanding productions during the rest of the year. The ENO sings in English (which purists hate) but they eschew Mozart in favour of works that have often been unjustly forgotten, reviving operas that are often colourful, humorous and compelling, presented with flair.

Royal Albert Hall (*Kensington Gore; tel: 0891 500252*). For most people, the Albert Hall means one thing: the **Henry Wood Promenade Concerts**, which run every summer, from July to September. You won't stand a chance of getting into the big events without booking weeks in advance, but most other concerts have last-minute tickets available, and you can always queue for cheap standing tickets in the arena or gallery and be a true promenader.

Royal Festival Hall (*South Bank; tel: (020) 7633 0932*). With three concert halls to fill (RFH1 is what used to be known as the Festival Hall, now used for orchestral concerts; RFH2 and RFH3 were the smaller Queen Elizabeth Hall and Purcell Room, used for chamber concerts and recitals, respectively), every night brings a varied programme of events to this South Bank complex, with literary readings, folk and jazz on the menu, as well as classical concerts, plus free foyer concerts and photographic exhibitions.

Royal National Theatre (*South Bank; tel: (020) 7452 3400*). Worth a visit just for the views from the terrace café, this is the theatre that bears the standard for British acting, directorship and production: classics (mainly 20th-century) are interspersed with experimental works and even some popular musicals.

Royal Opera House (*Covent Garden; tel: (020) 7240 1200*). Once the symbol of all things corporate and snobbish, the ROH is working hard to earn new democratic credentials, with a range of cheaper tickets aimed at allowing ordinary mortals to experience the cream of British ballet and operatic talent.

Sadler's Wells (*Rosebery Avenue; tel: (020) 7863 8000*). World-class opera, ballet and contemporary touring productions in a newly built theatre that enjoys excellent acoustics and sightlines.

Shakespeare's Globe (*New Globe Walk; tel: (020) 7401 9919*). Authentic productions in the open air in a reconstruction of the original theatre for which Shakespeare's plays were written. Instead of the riotous apprentices who attended Shakespeare's original plays, the audience now consists of students and coach parties.

The alternative scene

London's thriving alternative arts scene is documented weekly in listings magazines such as *Time Out*, or weekend newspaper supplements. Small theatres, clubs and venues all over London are the crucibles in which talented artists test and hone their skills before emerging into the mainstream. As a backlash against the po-faced Pinteresque school of experimental drama, comedy and cabaret are thriving: who wouldn't rather have a good laugh than sit through someone's tedious and unstructured ravings, no matter how therapeutic for the soul. Top venues include the **Comedy Store** (*Haymarket House, 1a Oxenden Street; tel: (01426) 914433; performances Tue–Sun at 2000, Fri and Sat at midnight*) and **Jongleurs** (*Dingwalls, Middle Yard, Camden Lock; tel: (020) 7564 2500; performances Fri and Sat; for the rest of the week, Jongleurs offers live Indie bands 1930 to midnight*), one of a chain of comedy clubs with a bar, food and disco.

Practical information

PRACTICAL INFORMATION

Practical information

Airports

London is served by five international airports: Heathrow, Gatwick, Luton, Stansted and London City, all close to the capital. Transport links into the city centre vary in quality:

Heathrow: The **Heathrow Express train** (*tel: 0845 600 1515; www.heathrowexpress.co.uk*) travels into Paddington Station every 15 minutes, with a 15-minute journey time. This is the quickest way into town and runs daily from 0502–2347.

A cheaper option is the **London Underground** (*tel: (020) 7222 1234; travinfo@londontransport.co.uk*), which runs every 10 minutes or so daily from about 0530 to 2330. The journey from Heathrow to Piccadilly Circus on the Piccadilly line takes about 60 minutes. Alternatively, the **Airbus** service (*tel: (020) 8400 6665; www.airbus.co.uk*) has three buses an hour to 15 destinations in central London and a journey time of 60 to 90 minutes. **Taxi** fares are pricey and should be avoided unless your luggage is unmanageable.

Gatwick: The **Gatwick Express** service (*tel: 0990 301530*) to Victoria Station runs every 15 minutes between 0500 and midnight and then hourly. It gets you into London in about 30 minutes. **Connex South Central** (*tel: 0345 484950*) runs trains into Victoria around the clock. They depart every 5–10 minutes, take 30 minutes and are the cheapest train option. If you want to go by road try the **Jetlink 777 bus** (*tel: 0990 747777*) into Victoria Coach Station via five key London destinations. The buses take about 1 hour and 15 minutes and run daily and hourly from 0500–2010. **Taxis** can take 1 to 2 hours to reach your destination – forget it unless you have money to burn!

Stansted: The **Stansted Express** (*tel: 0345 484950*) leaves for Liverpool Street Station every 15 minutes daily between 0600 and midnight and takes 45 minutes. **Jetlink 777 buses** (*tel: 0990 747777*) go to Victoria Coach Station between 0800 and 1800 every hour, then two-hourly in the evening until 2215, taking roughly 1 hour and 45 minutes. **Taxis** are the expensive option.

Luton: Your best bet is to catch a shuttle bus (every 15 minutes) to Luton Airport Parkway Station and take a **Thameslink train** (*tel: 0345 484950*). There are 4 trains an hour and they take 30 minutes to get to King's Cross Station. Otherwise **Greenline coaches** (*tel: (020) 8668 7261*) travel half-hourly between 0930 and 1915, then hourly, into Victoria Coach Station. They run daily 24 hours a day and take about one and a half hours. **Taxis** are expensive with erratic journey times because of heavy traffic.

London City: Take a shuttlebus (every 5–7 minutes) to the **Silverlink Metro** (*tel: 0345 484950*). Trains run every 30 minutes and connect up with the tube. The **Airbus** service (*tel: (020) 7222 1234*) or the **Airport shuttlebus** (*tel: (020) 7646 0088*) take 30 minutes to get to Liverpool Street, leaving every 10 minutes throughout the day. **Taxis** take about 30–40 minutes.

Climate

The British weather is everyone's favourite topic of conversation! The weather in London is very **variable**. The best plan is to check the newspaper, radio or TV forecasts but be prepared for rain. In summer May and June can be bitterly cold or they can be warm and sunny. July and August are the only months when you can count on sunshine and when the sun does come out, temperatures rise to between 25° and 28°C. In winter temperatures sink

to 10°C or below: sun, wind and rain are the main ingredients but frost and snow are rare in London, which has its own microclimate, several degrees warmer than the rest of England because of the heat pumped out by buildings, traffic and people. Spring and autumn are mixed and temperatures average at about 15°C. Notorious rainy months are April, late September and November; however, rain in mid-summer is common too. *Weathercall: tel: 0891 500401 or www.weather.com.*

Currency

British pounds sterling (£) are divided into 100 (pence). Notes come in **denominations** of £5, £10, £20 and £50. Coins come in 1p, 2p, 5p, 10p, 20p, 50p, £1 and £2 denominations. You can import as much cash as you like. **ATMs** (Automatic Teller Machines) are widespread. Many hotels and most banks and bureaux de change will change **travellers' cheques**. **Credit cards** are accepted in almost all shops, restaurants and tourist attractions. **Prices** are nearly always quoted inclusive of VAT.

When changing money, use a bank for the best rates, or a reputable bureaux de change, such as Thomas Cook. Many London bureaux de change advertise apparently attractive rates and then charge a hefty commission, or they advertise 'no-commission' and give you a poor rate. Hotels give the poorest rates of all. It is easy to be taken in by misleading advertising, so make sure you know exactly what you are in for before changing money or travellers' cheques.

Customs Regulations

Citizens of the EU may bring unrestricted amounts of goods into the country as long as they are not duty-free and are for their personal use. However, if you are a **non-EU member** or if you have bought **duty-free** goods, then the following restrictions apply:

- 200 cigarettes or 50 cigars
- 2 litres of wine
- 2 litres of still table wine plus either 2 litres of alcohol under 22% proof or 1 litre of alcohol over 22% proof
- 60ml of perfume
- 250ml of toilette water
- other goods up to the value of £32

Electricity

The current in the UK is 240 volts. Plugs have 3 square prongs. **Adaptors** are available at airports and chemists. Shaving sockets take 2-pin plugs and are 110 volts.

Entry formalities

For all EU citizens and many others, including those from the USA, Canada, Australia, New Zealand or South Africa visiting for short holidays, **only a passport** is needed. Other nationalities should **check entry requirements** *before* travelling.

Health and insurance

It is recommended that you take out comprehensive **travel insurance**.

Free emergency medical treatment under the National Health Service (NHS) is available to EU citizens, provided you equip yourself with the necessary forms in advance of your visit. Some other countries have reciprocal arrangements, but check before you travel as you may need documentation to claim free health care. Paying visitors can go privately or by NHS. Keep receipts for insurance purposes.

In an **emergency dial 999** for police, ambulance or fire services.

Chemists can give advice on minor ailments. Remember that your usual drugs may not be available for purchase over the counter, so bring an adequate supply.

Information

There is a wealth of information available: maps, books, magazines, newspapers and leaflets can be found in tourist offices, **bookshops**, street kiosks and **newsagents** such as WHSmith.

Tourist Information Offices

Heathrow Airport Terminals 1, 2, 3. *Tube station. Open: daily 0830–1800.*

Liverpool Street Station. *Tube station. Open: Mon–Fri 0800–1800, Sat and Sun 0845–1730.*

Victoria Station. *Station forecourt. Open: daily 0800–1900.*

Waterloo Station. *Arrivals hall. Open: daily 0800–2230.*

London Tourist Board. *www.londontown.com*. Useful for up-to-the-minute information on the many new attractions that are opening over the coming months and years in connection with the millennium or funded by the National Lottery.

Other information sources

The original – and still the world's best – listings magazine, **Time Out** gives you the low-down on everything that is happening in the capital, from comedy clubs to gay discos, from street markets to jazz clubs and bars, plus every play, dance and opera performance, art exhibition and film on show that week, all mixed in with dependable reviews and witty articles on life in the capital.

Other publications worth a look include the *Evening Standard* and the weekend supplements of national newspapers, such as *The Independent* or *Sunday Times*.

Londoners tune into **Capital Radio** on 95.8FM or **GLR** (Greater London Radio) on 94.9FM to find out more about local events.

Visitor Call has up-to-date information about events for tourists. *Tel: 0839 123456.*

Kidsline gives you fresh ideas to entertain the children. *Tel: (020) 7222 8070.*

Maps

The tube map and the street maps in this guide will get you happily round London but, if you want a more detailed map, the ***London A–Z*** guide is the most comprehensive you can buy and it is available in newsagents and bookshops all over London.

Opening times

Most shops, restaurants, bars and tourist sights are open daily, with only slightly shorter opening hours on Sundays.

Shops trade from roughly 1000 (some open as early as 0900) until 1800 in the main tourist areas. Some larger stores have late night trading – Wednesdays (Knightsbridge and Chelsea) or Thursdays (West End) – and stay open until 2000. On Sundays, shops are only allowed to open for six hours, so most opt for 1000–1600 or 1200–1800.

Banks normally open Monday to Friday 0930–1700 and 0930–1230 Saturday mornings. Out of hours you can use your credit or debit card to obtain cash from cash-point machines.

Museums and **galleries** usually open Monday to Saturday 1000–1800 and on Sunday 1400–1800.

Restaurant and **bar** opening times vary according to the establishment. Many pubs now stay open all day.

Public Holidays

Most offices close on a 'Bank Holiday'. That said, you still find many shops, restaurants, bars and petrol stations trading, except on Christmas Day, Boxing Day and New Year's Day. If the holiday falls on a weekend then it is held over until the following Monday.

The main Bank Holidays in England are:

1 January
New Year's Day

Friday before Easter Day
Good Friday

Monday after Easter Day
Easter Monday

First Monday in May
May Day

Last Monday in May
Spring Bank Holiday

Last Monday in August
Late Summer Bank Holiday

25 December
Christmas Day

26 December
Boxing Day

Reading and films

Novels such as Charles Dickens' *Bleak House* and *Oliver Twist*, Sir Arthur Conan Doyle's Sherlock Holmes stories and Virginia Woolf's *Mrs Dalloway* conjure up evocative scenes of old London. Others give a taste of angst-ridden, modern, middle-class London in novels such as *Jemima J* by Jane Green or *Ralph's Party* by Lisa Jewell. Hanif Kureishi's *The Buddha of Suburbia* and Martin Amis' *London Fields* take a satirical view of the London suburbs and East London low-life.

Films that portray middle-class London include *Notting Hill*, starring the foppish Hugh Grant and elegant Julia Roberts. Grim Victorian London comes to life in *The Elephant Man* and *Little Dorrit*. *The World is Not Enough*, the 1999 James Bond film, is the latest to use London as the backdrop for its opening action sequence.

Safety and Security

Walking around central London is generally safe, although you should always stay alert, particularly in crowded places. **Pickpockets** will make a beeline for any grabbable wallets or cameras, so be sensible with your belongings and don't become side-tracked. The best advice is to look confident, rather than lost. If in doubt, get out!

At night steer clear of unlit streets and parks as these can be pretty creepy, especially in some suburbs. Public transport at night is relatively safe but stay in the more crowded areas. Only use black taxis and not unregistered, private cars.

Report stolen cards or cheques to the issuing company and stolen passports to your embassy or consulate. Report all crimes to the **police** and get a copy of their report for insurance.

Telephones

Most of the ubiquitous red phone boxes have disappeared from the streets to be replaced by perspex British Telecom and Mercury boxes.

You will find these on the streets, in tube, rail and bus stations, restaurants, bars and department stores.

Boxes take **phonecards**, **coins** or **credit cards** (some take all three). Phonecards are usually available from post offices, newsagents or street kiosks. BT ones can be slotted into any BT payphone; there are, however, universal phonecards, such as the WHSmith phonecard, which can be used in any phone. These have a freephone number and a PIN number to call and input before dialling. All boxes have dialling instructions.

Most phone companies operate **peak** (0800–1800) and **off-peak** (rest of the time) calling times.

To make an **international call** dial 00, then the access code of the country you are calling (eg, Australia = 61), then the area code (minus the initial 0), followed by the local number.

Useful numbers

Emergency services	999
Operator	100
Directory Enquiries	192

All London numbers changed area codes on 22 April 2000, so if you encounter an out-of-date number, use the following new codes:

Central London
instead of **0171**, use **0207**
Outer London
instead of **0181**, use **0208**.

Time

London is the home of **Greenwich**, the base for calculating the world's time. London uses Greenwich Meantime (GMT) from October to March, then switches to GMT plus one hour for British Summer Time, which lasts from the last Sunday in March to the last Sunday in October.

Tipping

Restaurants often include service in the final bill, so in theory you should not need to leave a further tip. In reality you will find a great deal of pressure to do so: you will be presented with an open credit card slip on to which you have to write the final amount, a non-too-subtle invitation to add a further amount, or your waiter will manage to insinuate that a personal tip, as distinct from the one that goes to management, would be appreciated.

Many people have tried to wage war against the whole iniquitous business of tipping, but the battle has not yet been won (not helped by the fact that American visitors seem to think it necessary to tip everyone who crosses their path). You will have to choose whether to use your strength of character to defy the system single handed, or go with the flow.

In the smarter London bars barmen often give change on a saucer, hoping that you'll leave it there! Coffee bars and sandwich bars, public and private toilets and museum cloakroom attendants are also in on the act, with a strategically placed saucer labelled 'for the staff'. Pubs are one of the few places where tipping is still rarely expected.

Taxi drivers will be abusive if they are not tipped a minimum of 10 per cent. Hairdressers and beauticians expect a similar percentage. It is always appropriate to tip tour guides, especially if they have been entertaining. If you are staying in a hotel with pretensions, it is likely that the porter and the doormen will expect tips if they hail a taxi or handle your luggage, as will room service, chamber maids and cloakroom attendants. All would expect about £1, as would railway porters (on top of their fee).

Toilets

Coin-operated **automated cabins** are springing up all over the place. You will find them in tourist areas and close to the entrances to tube and railway stations. All formal tourist attractions have toilets. If you want to get away without paying, the best bet is to go to a department store. Alternatively, all bars, pubs and restaurants will have toilets, but exclusively for the use of their customers.

Travellers with disabilities

Accessibility to most major sights, hotels and shops in London is relatively good for disabled visitors. Transport facilities are generally poor, especially on the tube, although some modern buses have good access. A comprehensive guide on all aspects of life for the disabled is ***Access in London***, published by Quiller. **Artsline** on *(020) 7388 2227* gives information on the accessibility of all arts venues. **Holiday Care Service** advises on accommodation (*tel: (01293) 774535*). **Tripscope** (*tel: (020) 8994 9294*) helps with getting around London.

Index

A

B

C

D

E

F

G

H

I

J

K

Editorial, design and production credits

Project management: Dial House Publishing

Series editor: Christopher Catling

Copy editor: Lucy Thomson

Proof-reader: Kate Owen

Series and cover design: Trickett & Webb Limited

Cover artwork: Wenham Arts

Text layout: Wenham Arts

Map work: PS Cartography

Repro and image setting: Z2 Repro, Thetford, Norfolk, UK

Printed and bound by: Artes Graficas ELKAR S. Coop., Bilbao, Spain

Acknowledgements

We would like to thank Ethel Davies for the photographs used in this book, to whom the copyright in the photographs belongs, with the exception of the following:

Page 63: Madame Tussaud's

Page 68: Liberty plc

Page 102: The Theatre Museum.